GETTING WORK DONE
ON YOUR HOUSE

a Consumer Publication

edited by Edith Rudinger
draft by Phil Parnham
illustrations by Jo Bampton

published by Consumers' Association
publishers of **Which?**

Which? Books are commissioned and researched
by The Association for Consumer Research
and published by Consumers' Association,
2 Marylebone Road, London NW1 4DX and
Hodder and Stoughton, 47 Bedford Square,
London WC1B 3DF

© Consumers' Association Ltd September 1988

ISBN 0 340 48935 9
and   0 85202 403 7

Photoset by Paston Press, Loddon, Norfolk
Printed and bound at the University Printing House, Oxford

GETTING WORK DONE
ON YOUR HOUSE

a Consumer Publication

Consumers' Association
publishers of **Which?**
2 Marylebone Road
London NW1 4DX

4

Contents

Foreword

A high percentage of the housing in this country is over 70 years old and the condition of many properties is getting worse rather than better. Property owning also means property maintaining. Home improvements and domestic building work for individual home owners now form a significant percentage of the construction industry's turnover.

But home owners have not always been pleased with the construction industry's response. Everyone has heard tales of unreliable builders, shoddy work, over-charging, cowboy contractors taking thousands of pounds off their customers, repaired roofs that continue to leak, loft conversions that collapse, work that is never finished.

Many people may know what they would like to do to their house to improve or maintain it but have put off doing so, unable to face the hassle and anxiety, uncertainty about the eventual expense, the potential frustration and disappointment, that 'getting the builders in' may entail. When a building scheme goes wrong, the impact on householder and family can be overwhelming.

Because the building process is very technical, many lay people find it totally mystifying and confusing — a factor that some builders and professionals have used to their advantage. The cowboys flourish, encouraged by the ignorance and gullibility of the public, who have no sure means of distinguishing the fake fly-by-night from the experienced contractor of integrity.

In response to criticism and complaints, the construction industry has begun to improve its public image. Trade organisations and professional associations realise that it is in their own interests to provide some customer protection and guarantee of members' work. But this development is as yet slow and patchy, offering only limited security for the customer. The best defence for ordinary householders remains their own resourcefulness.

This book explains in straightforward terms the procedure for getting building work done so as to help the ordinary person to take more control and avoid some of the disasters that have befallen many people in the past. It offers some guidelines to help you choose a reliable team to carry out the work you've decided on. It deals with the situation of using a professional as designer and co-ordinator of your scheme and with the more vulnerable situation of going it alone and employing a builder on your own.

Throughout this book

for 'he' read 'he or she'

Who this book is for

The disadvantage of defining the type of person for whom a book is written is that those who don't strictly fit within that category but who also may find it useful probably won't bother to read on.

The book has been written for the ordinary home owner who wants to employ a builder to carry out various works on his or her property. It assumes that this typical person has no particular knowledge or experience of the building industry and has only basic DIY skills. The book covers both small and more substantial building projects as well as emergency repair works. It deals with schemes organised by a professional on your behalf and those where you employ a builder directly.

A 'professional' in this context is a person with qualifications and/or experience which, among other matters, enable him or her to advise on the feasibility of improvement or repair work on a house, to design the project if required, to draw up the technical specifications and the contract, to arrange for and inspect the actual building work. This function is separate from that of the builder or other specialist contractor — who may be equally 'professional' within his own category. For simplicity throughout most of this book, the advisory/supervisory person is generically referred to as "the professional": he or she may be an architect, a surveyor, a designer, an architectural technician, a design consultant — or be called by one of any number of related titles.

This book does not aim to turn you into a builder or an architect or surveyor; it aims to help you become an informed client, who can play a helpful and constructive role in any scheme, while at the same time protecting your own interests.

The key to this is preparation. If you don't get ready for the project, you'll stand less chance of keeping it on the rails. A few hours spent reading, researching and discussing early on will save you time, heartache and money later.

the types of work

The variety of work organised by home owners on their property is considerable. This book is non-specific and can be applied to different schemes.

Generally, most building schemes on domestic property can be divided into two categories

○ maintenance and repair
○ improvements and additions.

Here are a few examples of types of work commonly carried out.

maintenance and repair

○ repairing/replacing roof slates, tiles, chimneys, guttering
○ repointing brickwork, repairing external rendering

o underpinning failed foundations, rebuilding collapsing walls
o repairing/renewing windows and doors
o eradicating dry rot, replacing floor joists etc
o eradicating rising damp, with associated replastering
o replastering old walls and ceilings
o repainting externally and redecorating internally
o repairing/replacing boilers, heaters, defective pipework, baths, toilets, basins
o rewiring electrical circuits, replacing old gas mains and pipework
o renewing fences, paths, garden walls.

improvements and additions

o new garage
o new conservatory, house extension or loft conversion
o fitting a new kitchen or bathroom
o internal alterations such as knocking two rooms into one, dividing one large room into two, open plan staircase
o applying new cladding or other exterior treatments
o installing central heating.

The list is endless and depends totally on circumstances. One thing the works all have in common is that a general builder or one of the more common specialist contractors will be required to carry them out.

This book will not tell you what sort of repair to carry out or what type of improvement will be most suitable. That's for you to sort out. But, once you have decided, it tells you how to get someone to carry out the work on your behalf.

Remember - your property is probably your greatest asset. Repairs and maintenance are essential; extensions and renovations can be monetarily rewarding. Do not put off essential repairs just because organising them would be inconvenient and getting work done on your home could be traumatic.

Hire a professional or organise it yourself?

One of the main decisions to take is whether you will employ a professional person (such as an architect or a surveyor) to organise the work for you or whether you will do the organising yourself.

There are no easy answers — it will depend on a number of varying factors:

○ the complexity of the scheme
○ the cost of the scheme
○ your own knowledge/experience
○ your available time and degree of commitment.

the complexity of the scheme
If the scheme is likely to be very technically complex and you feel that you won't have a chance of understanding it, let alone organising it, you should consider calling in a professional. For instance, your project may involve building a dining room or lounge extension or a loft conversion and require planning permission as well as building regulations approval. It is

advisable that you don't attempt to be in charge, unless you have sufficient experience of this type of work.

Conversely, if the project consists of a number of repairs or improvements that you are reasonably familiar with and you've had experience of employing a builder before, then possibly you could have a go at being in charge.

the cost of the scheme
The amount the scheme is likely to cost need not be a factor in your decision. A complicated scheme may be relatively cheap but need a professional whereas a large redecorating job may cost a lot but be relatively easy to organise. Where finance is being borrowed for the project, your lender may insist on your getting professional advice.

your own knowledge/experience
If you've organised building work before, even it it's only been a small amount, you will be more prepared than someone starting from fresh. Even if your experience has not been with building contractors, if you have been involved in a 'consumer' contract previously with another type of firm, you may have picked up a few pointers than can be applied to the construction industry.

your available time
No matter how smoothly the scheme might go, it is likely to involve a lot of your time. If you have a lot of commitments at work, socially, with the family or you don't fancy spending your spare time doing this sort of thing, you should think about bringing in a professional. Even so, you will be spending a lot of time watching the professional.

test yourself

When trying to decide whether you should employ a professional or do it yourself, you could have a go at this little quiz: it may help you to focus on the issues involved, whatever your score.

(It would be better if you read through the book and then return to this section as some of the questions relate to the discussions in other chapters.)

Answer all the questions truthfully, choosing the option that's nearest to your own position. Add up the scores at the end and see how you do.

1. COMPLEXITY
How technically complicated is your project likely to be:

a. does it involve foundation work, building new walls, knocking holes in or removing existing walls, altering roof structure, drainage?
b. is it mainly maintenance work such as replastering, re-roofing, replumbing, rewiring, guttering and rainwater pipes replacement, redecorations etc?

2. PERMISSIONS
Is the scheme likely to need:

a. planning permission and/or building regulations approval?
b. neighbours' agreement e.g. to 'party wall' work?
c. no permission required.

3. COSTS
How much do you think your scheme will cost:

a. above £5000
b. between £1000 and £5000
c. below £1000

4. PREVIOUS EXPERIENCE

Have you ever been involved in organising building work before:

a. never
b. yes, but only a small amount
c. yes, quite a sizeable scheme e.g. new rear extension to house, reroofing, improvement grant work.

5. TECHNICAL KNOWLEDGE

How would you describe your knowledge of technical matters in the building industry such as construction and repair methods and materials:

a. very little or no knowledge
b. a reasonable knowledge of basic DIY skills: you can put up a shelf, change a tap washer, repaint window frames, etc.
c. extensive knowledge i.e. work within the building industry, knowledge of construction practices, extensive DIY experience.

6. CONSUMER MATTERS

How much experience have you had in dealing with 'consumer' problems e.g. taking defective items back to shops, complaining about defective work or incompetent service:

a. none or very little
b. a reasonable amount but mainly face to face or simple correspondence
c. extensive experience involving letter writing, understanding contracts, taking consumer/legal advice and even small scale county court action.

7. COPING WITH STRESS

How would you describe your ability to cope with problem situations:

a. Good. You handle them quite well and are not easily over-whelmed by other people. You are reasonably assertive and don't mind standing your ground when necessary.
b. Although you don't like getting involved in arguments, you know when to draw the line and defend your position.
c. You don't like face to face conflict and tend to accept things when you know you should not. You have a tendency to get worked up very quickly when things go wrong.

SCORES

1. a) 3   b) 1
2. a) 4   b) 2   c) 1
3. a) 3   b) 2   c) 1
4. a) 3   b) 2   c) 1
5. a) 3   b) 2   c) 1
6. a) 3   b) 2   c) 1
7. a) 1   b) 2   c) 3

HOW DID YOU DO?

High score - let's face it, you aren't exactly Sir Christopher Wren. People have a variety of skills and abilities, yours are clearly not in the building sphere. You should seriously consider employing a professional for all but the most straightforward maintenance items. Your lack of experience and knowledge of the building process will leave you vulnerable and you would find a large scheme difficult to control by yourself.

Medium score - you're half way there. You should stand a fair chance of organising building work successfully, but if any problems crop up, you'll probably flounder a bit. If you do go it alone, you will have to work hard.

Low score - you're a professional in all but name! You should stand a reasonable chance of coping with the pressures that organising a building scheme would bring. If you need drawings done for building regulations and/or planning permis-

layout and design of buildings including decorations and furnishings.

The RIBA runs a Clients' Advisory Service in London and at regional offices, from which you can get a list of architects suitable for particular categories of work. The RIBA 's promotional leaflet *Working with your architect* giving advice on smaller building projects, suggests you telephone each of the architects on your list to determine which would be interested in your project and make an appointment with the most likely-sounding ones to discuss the possibilities further.

For Scotland, the RIAS has a leaflet *Get it right first time* regarding the services of architects, and can provide a directory of suitable architects' firms with details of their experience.

surveyors

The term 'chartered surveyor' is legally protected and can be used only by members of the professional institution — **The Royal Institution of Chartered Surveyors (RICS).** The general title 'surveyor' is not protected, so anyone can use that.

Chartered surveyors with ARICS or FRICS after their name come in a number of varieties. They could range from auctioneers through to the coordinators of large building investment projects on behalf of pension funds. So, employing someone just because he is 'ARICS' can be a bit of a lucky dip. You should find out what variety of surveyor he is.

The Institution is split into different divisions, of which the General Practice Division, perhaps the Quantity Surveyors Division, and the Building Surveyors Division, are the ones that householders and members of the general public are more likely to be dealing with.

Members of the General Practice Division are usually

employed as valuers for building societies or as estate agents not only buying and selling houses and land but also managing property on behalf of landlords. They will carry out structural surveys/housebuyers reports and organise the maintenance and repair of property they are managing.

Surveyors in the Building Surveyors Division are more technically oriented with knowledge and experience of technical and legal matters which may be applied to a wide variety of work. Some chartered building surveyors are trained to deal with repairs, alterations, extensions and adaptations to existing buildings. These are the ones you should look for.

The RICS has an information centre which suggests names of appropriate chartered surveyor firms in any given area, from the membership database.

composite professional institutions

There are other professional bodies whose members are qualified by examination and assessment to carry out structural surveys and/or to give architectural advice and organise building work.

Faculty of Architects and Surveyors
designatory letters: for surveyor members, FFS (fellow), AFS (associate); for architect members FFAS, AFAS; for architectural technicians, LFS.

Incorporated Association of Architects and Surveyors
designatory letters: for surveyor members FIAS (fellow), MIAS (member); for architect members FIAA, MIAA; for dual role, FIAA&S, MIAA&S; for associate technician members AMIAS.

Incorporated Society of Valuers and Auctioneers
designatory letters: FSVA (fellow), ASVA (associate); of the divisions within ISVA, the general practice division is the one the householder is most likely to be dealing with.

All the organisations have an investigatory procedure for any lapse in professional conduct and for complaints from clients. Names of their members in any given area are available from the appropriate head office or regional branch (see local telephone directory) or a directory of members may be in the local reference library.

other professionals

Architects and surveyors are the most common professionals used by householders, but you may come across others.

technicians

Professional institutions are the **Society of Surveying Technicians** (designatory letters MSST) and the **British Institute of Architectural Technicians** (designatory letters MBIAT).

In many surveying offices, technicians as well as architects and chartered surveyors will be encountered, in some cases in partnership with professional principals. The technicians put general ideas into practice; they take the designs and add the detail to turn them into workable schemes. Some technicians become so experienced that they end up doing the job of an architect or a surveyor but without the status. Many technicians have set up on their own and become self-employed. You may find that they are more prepared to get involved with domestic projects than their other professional counterparts — and tend to be cheaper.

structural engineers

The professional body is the **Institution of Structural Engineers** (designatory letters for chartered structural engineer members C.Eng. MIStructE or C.Eng.FIStructE; for technician members TEng. AMIStructE).

Structural engineering is generally taken to be a specialist discipline within the construction industry, overlapping with the skills of the architect, the surveyor and the building services engineer. A structural engineer usually works as part of a design team. For instance, the architect may produce a design and the engineer specifies the beams, columns, floors and foundations that hold the whole thing up. The householder will come into contact with one in a limited set of circumstances:

○ Where an architect is organising a scheme on your house and a large opening has to be created in a wall, the architect may suggest that a structural engineer is employed to calculate and design the beam that will be needed.
○ If your foundations have failed or a wall is buckling, a structural engineer may be the best person to call in.

choosing your professional

Identifying the sort of professional who will best suit your project is step one in choosing a person or firm to take on the work. You should have an interview with whoever you believe might be suitable, in order to discuss your ideas and get his or her reactions. You should also find out about their membership of a professional body and about their indemnity insurance, and ask for references.

insurance

Over the last few years, legal actions against professionals, such as surveyors and architects, for negligence have been well publicised. Most professionals have carried 'professional indemnity' insurance cover for many years, in order to ensure that adequate funds were always available to meet successful claims in negligence. Professional indemnity insurance is now mandatory for members of the Incorporated Society of Valuers and Auctioneers, of the Royal Institution of Chartered Surveyors and of the Faculty of Architects. More recently, some of the other professional associations have arranged full professional indemnity insurance schemes or policies for their members to take out. The cost of these policies relates to the value and type of work carried out by the particular professional and in some cases can be quite expensive; many small firms and one-man-bands find it too expensive.

You should ask any professional whether he is covered by indemnity insurance and to tell you what sort of cover it provides. But some insurance companies forbid policy holders to disclose insurance details to clients.

references

Recent work undertaken by the professional is a good indicator of his skills. Most will be happy to provide you with a list of clients they have done work for. Ask specifically for names of private individuals rather than firms or public bodies, who have had schemes similar to yours done. Names of past or existing clients and details of work undertaken will not be disclosed without prior approval of that client.

Professionals who work for substantial clients and prefer not to take instructions from private householders will make this quite clear, but can usually be relied on to recommend a fellow professional who will be pleased to accept the work.

The type of client that they usually work for is an important factor. Many professionals prefer to work for public clients or do only major projects for private ones, which provide larger, more interesting and profitable jobs than the average householder can provide. Some see private individuals as 'uneducated' clients taking up their time for a relatively small fee. Despite this, many professionals still take on this type of work from time to time.

Some firms, on the other hand, see work for householders as their 'bread and butter' and welcome such appointments. It is this type of professional you should be aiming to get. Taking up references and finding out the type of client they have worked for will help to reveal this.

working alone

Many professionals work on their own: through necessity or choice, they have set up in a sole practice. Many have excellent records and carry out good work but there are a number of points you should clarify:
- what are the arrangements if the person is ill or on holiday, who will look after the work?
- how easy is it to contact him? Does he have an office and a secretary or does he work from home and have an answering machine?

Again, one of the ways to check the suitability of a one-man-bander is by talking to a previous client.

weekenders

Some professional individuals, whether they work for private firms or public bodies, traditionally do jobs 'on the side' in their spare time, usually for cash. Typical jobs include drawing up plans for garages, extensions, loft conversions and sometimes a little supervision of a building project. They usually do this work for family, friends or 'friends of friends' at a price that undercuts the going rate for that type of work. Although the cost may be attractive, you should think carefully about entering into such an agreement because

○ the individual almost certainly will not have any profes-sional indemnity insurance to cover private jobs, so if any-thing went wrong, you would have to sue the individual and would be unlikely to recover adequate compensation

○ as he is working in his spare time, he may not be able to meet your deadlines, or progress the work evenly, or supervise it

○ he may be reluctant to commit much to paper, and this could create the opportunity for misunderstandings and disputes.

Employing a friend can also be problematic even if you appoint him properly. If things begin to go wrong, relation-ships could become difficult and embarrassing.

location

Although many professionals work at great distances from their office base, it is best to try and employ one who is locally based. This is because

○ it will be easier for him to keep an eye on the work. Although all professionals should inspect projects properly, whatever the distance, there is more chance of regular inspections if you are only down the road rather than many miles away.

○ a separate charge may be made for travelling expenses and other 'disbursements'. These will obviously be higher the farther the person has to come, especially if he has to stay overnight in a hotel.

○ knowledge of the local area can be invaluable. For instance, familiarity with local construction methods, soil conditions, building contractors and local authority procedures and personnel will be useful.

what will his services cost?

One of the first things you need to discuss with a professional adviser is the fee he is likely to charge for his services. This will depend on the extent of the services you want him to provide as well as on his fee structure. The RICS, RIBA and FAS have produced guidelines for the fees to be charged by their members. These fee structures are for guidance only as it would be illegal for the institutions to promote them as fixed fees to be charged by all members.

basis for charging

The recommended charges are based on a percentage of the total construction cost of the work being organised. The actual percentage will depend on

○ the nature of the project
○ the value of the proposed work.

Higher fees are charged for projects on existing buildings than for those involving new building. This reflects not so much the higher levels of time, skill and knowledge demanded by refurbishment contracts but compensates for the greater amount of time spent by the professional relative to the construction cost.

Both the RIBA and RICS recommend higher fees for small value contracts on the homes of private individuals because the percentage fee on very small projects does not adequately recompense the professional. In these cases, a lump-sum fee should be agreed. Some professionals will negotiate charges based on an hourly rate rather than a percentage fee. In any event, agree exactly what service will be given for what fee.

basic services

Assuming that a professional adviser works for the conventional percentage fee to design and oversee a building project on your house, this will buy what is called 'basic services'. This covers the types of task than an average architect/surveyor should be carrying out during an average contract, split into different stages.

The RIBA's document *Architect's appointment* (£2 from RIBA Publications, Finsbury Mission, Moreland Street, London EC1V 8BB) sets out the services an architect may offer, the conditions which normally apply, recommended fees and expenses, with an example of an agreement plus schedule that could be used. There is an abbreviated version for small works (up to £100,000), price £1. (Similar documents are available for architects' appointments in Scotland from the Royal Incorporation of Architects in Scotland.)

The stages set out in the RIBA's *Architect's appointment* provide the client as well as the professional with a good checklist.

Work stages A and B relate to preliminary services of discussion, inspection and suggestions and advice on feasibility.

work stage C — outline proposals
Your requirements are discussed and a basic scheme with cost estimates is drawn up for your approval.

work stage D — scheme design
A design is built up and refined so that you can start taking decisions over sizes, materials, appearance etc. A more accurate estimate of costs is produced and possible start and completion dates are discussed. Application for planning permission, if required, is made at this stage.

work stage E — detail design
Decisions about type of construction, quality of materials,

standard of workmanship are taken. Quotations for specialist work obtained, and cost checks made and reported back to you. Applications for building regulations approval and other statutory requirements are made.

Any major changes by you after this stage may cost extra if the professional has to amend the drawings.

work stages F and G — production information
Final drawings are produced and the specification put together in sufficient detail to go out to contractors for quotations.

work stage H — tendering
You will be advised on which contractors should be asked to quote for the job i.e. to 'tender'. Following your approval, the project will be tendered and when the prices are returned, they should be checked over and recommendations given to you as to which tender to accept.

work stage J — project planning
You will be advised on the contract to be signed between you and the chosen contractor.

work stage K — operations on site
The work actually starts and the professional checks that it is being done in accordance with the specification and drawings. You should receive regular financial reports especially if there are variations.

work stage L — completion
The professional ensures that the work is finished properly. You should be advised on maintenance of the completed work and receive drawings showing drainage and other services such as gas, electricity etc.

The payment of professional fees relates to these stages. The table opposite shows what proportion of the total fee the RIBA recommends for payment after each stage.

work stage	proportion of fee	cumulative total
C	15%	15%
D	20%	35%
E	20%	55%
F G	20%	75%
H J K L	25%	100%

A significant factor if the professional charges fees on this stages basis is that most of the fee (75%) becomes payable before work starts on site. This reflects the distribution of the workload and the professional's priorities. More time is spent before the commencement of the contract, on designing, defining, specifying and detailing the work, than on supervision or inspection on site.

On small projects you could try negotiating a slightly amended fee payment — say, 50% at stage F/G and 50% at completion. On many domestic jobs, the professional may even wait until the end of the job before payment is requested.

extra services

The recommended percentage fee is for 'basic services' only. If your scheme involves duties outside these defined services or you specifically ask for something extra, the professional may make additional charges over and above the percentage fee. These charges are usually based on a rate per hour. For example, if your whole house or site needs to be measured up in order to proceed with the design, or for submissions for approvals, the professional may charge this element on a time basis. Or if you live in a conservation area and it might prove difficult to get planning permission, your professional may think it necessary to have a meeting with the local authority's planning department before a planning application is made and may charge you separately for the time spent at the meeting. You should ask at an early stage what, if any, services will be charged in this way, and agree a budget limit for them.

Rates for charging on a time basis vary considerably but generally depend on the complexity of the work and the qualifications, experience and responsibility of the professional. When time charges are made, an accurate record of time spent should be kept by the professional and must be made available for your inspection, with reasonable notice.

partial services

Often a client wants only drawings done and planning permission and building regulations approval obtained. Most architects are prepared to undertake this and an hourly rate is generally most appropriate. The architect and client should both understand that their agreement ends then.

A professional adviser can save you money by preparing clear drawings and specification and getting competitive estimates from good builders. He may easily save the cost of his fees.

If you are not sure what to do with your property i.e. build an extension on it or convert the loft, you could ask the professional to carry out a feasibility study. This will help you analyse the available options and choose the one that's most appropriate. A feasibility study can be undertaken for a fixed fee.

repair and maintenance work
The Royal Institution of Chartered Surveyors suggests special standard charges to cover organising works of repair or maintenance. These cover taking particulars on site, writing specifications, obtaining estimates and administering the contract. Higher charges are made for smaller contracts.

other costs

Depending on the type and complexity of the scheme, some aspects of it may be beyond the skills of the professional adviser you have employed. For instance, assume that as part of the internal alterations, you want two rooms knocked into one and a special energy saving heating system installed. An architect may recommend that a structural engineer and a mechanical or heating engineer be employed to design these elements. These services will have to be paid by you in addition to the fee for the main professional. (An increasing number of architects are developing an expertise in energy effective design; so, if this is a feature of your scheme, try to find an architect with this kind of expertise at the outset.)

expenses

It is usual to have to pay for the out-of-pocket expenses of the professional and other 'disbursements' in connection with your scheme. These may include

○ printing and reproduction of all documents, maps, draw-ings, photos and other records
○ subsistence, hotel and travelling expenses including mileage allowance for cars at recognised rates
○ telex, telephone, fax, postal and other communication charges.

Not all of them will make charges for all of the above but most will claim for some. You should ask at an early stage what charges will be made, with an assessment of the likely cost of each.

statutory fees

If your scheme requires planning permission and/or building regulations approval, fees will have to be paid to the local authority. These are normally paid directly by the client i.e. you. For planning permission, a set fee is payable for an application. For building regulations approval, fees are on a scale based on the estimated cost of the project; for some extensions and loft conversions, it is a flat fee. VAT is payable on building regulations approval fees.

remember VAT

If the professional is registered for VAT (i.e. there is a registered number on the invoice), all the professional's charges will have VAT added to them at the standard rate (at present, 15%). This will add considerably to the total bill. If the professional is not registered, it may indicate that (a) he has just started business (b) he is part-time only or (c) he is not what he seems.

rise in costs

If the cost of the work rises, the professional has a duty to the client to clarify the reasons for this and to obtain approval to proceed, or to make savings elsewhere to compensate. The professional's fees on a percentage basis will go up proportionately to any rise in costs of the work.

If he is paid an hourly rate, the increase should reflect the additional time spent by the professional organising the extra work. For instance, if you decide you want a new kitchen fitting halfway through the contract, the professional will have to spend a lot of time designing and organising the work. On the other hand, if you decide to have the whole of your house redecorated rather than the three rooms originally planned, the professional won't have to do much work and so should not charge much extra.

paying the professional

Before appointing a professional adviser, you should always agree the terms and method of payment. It is wise to confirm this in writing. If it is a small job, he may well wait for payment until the end of the job. Others may insist on being paid according to the work stages. At the end of each work stage of the basic services, the professional may invoice you for the percentage of the fee as laid out in the table on page 39. This invoice could include

○ the appropriate percentage of the fee
○ the cost of employing any other professional
○ any statutory fees he may have paid on your behalf
○ any expenses he may have incurred up to that point on the above items apart from the statutory fees
○ VAT where applicable.

These payments should be made promptly unless you have very good reason not to. If you are unhappy with the service you are being given, be very careful before you start withholding payments: you may leave yourself open to legal action. If you do decide to withhold, it would be unfair to stop the whole payment if the professional let you down on only part of the service. Try to identify an appropriate amount.

If no fee is agreed between you and the professional, a 'reasonable' one will have to be paid. In this respect, the recommended scale of fees can be used in evidence.

what the professional does for you

To understand and control effectively a building scheme on your property for which you are employing a professional adviser, it is necessary to know what is meant to happen at the different stages of the project.

the briefing

The 'brief' is what you tell the professional you want out of the scheme. One reason why some professionals do not like working with householders on small projects is that they anticipate several changes of mind and a lot of wasted time before the 'brief' is agreed. This is where preparation pays off. Moreover, the professional will make an extra charge if these changes cause any redesign.

Before going to see the professional, you should write down an outline of what you want, to give to him. Keep a copy yourself and file it safely. If you have a good idea of your requirements, this stage will be relatively straightforward. The professional may have some initial comments and suggestions that might make your scheme more workable.

Be prepared for both professional and builder to pooh-pooh your ideas as "No one has that" or "Everybody does this". Stick to your guns unless your idea is proved totally impracticable or hazardous. They may be saying that because they don't want to bother with anything different.

initial survey

Whether the scheme is to be internal alterations/repairs, an extension or even a new building, the professional will have to carry out a survey of the proposed site.

It is important that a thorough survey is carried out of all the relevant features of the property so that the scheme includes all aspects of the work. You could ask the professional to extend the scope of the survey to a full structural survey, especially if you have not had one done within the last three years or so. Although this will give rise to an extra charge, it could identify further repairs or problems at an early stage. An 'as-existing' survey of your house should show up any cracks or existing dilapidations before any work starts. These should, if possible, be recorded and agreed with the builder in advance. Then, if the builder causes damage to other parts of your property by the way the work is done, he will have to put it right.

If the professional carries out only a superficial survey and doesn't notice a few cracks and unstable walls, these omissions may not become apparent until the builder has started work. This is when costs begin to rise and the contract may start to go wrong. If you, the professional and the builder are arguing about money and the extent of the work, other aspects of the job may begin to slip. The standard could become sloppy, progress slow up and the contract spiral downwards.

You can help by passing on all the information and knowledge you have about your property. For instance:

○ where access to the loft or cellar is (offer ladders or steps, if possible)
○ where the main services (gas, water, electricity) are
○ where the main drains and any inspection covers are
○ details of problems/defects that the property has suffered from in the past and any repairs that have been carried out either by yourself or by the previous owners. Details of any timber treatment and damp proof course work and associated guarantees should be given.

If original plans of the house exist, they will be useful. If not, before considering adding an extension or conservatory, you may need a professional to draw up plans of what exists at present. (In the case of a recent building, duplicates may be obtainable from the original builders.)

For some projects, it may help the survey if the structure could be 'opened up'. For example:

○ if your foundations have failed, the professional will probably ask for several holes to be dug around the base of the walls and in your garden to determine the reason for the fault

○ where dry rot has affected the timbers of the ground floor, it may be necessary to hack off some plaster to discover the true extent of the repairs needed

○ if you are having an opening formed in a structural wall, it may help the professional to design the finished scheme if you offer to lift the carpets and floorboards on the floor above.

The type and extent of these opening-up works will depend on the property and the type of project. Whether you could do it yourself or need to get in a builder will depend on your skills and resources. What you must remember is that the actual repair work probably won't start for several months so you may have to consider temporary 'making good' of the opened-up work. Such work may appear an unnecessary additional expense but it can save a lot of trouble and expense later on. Discuss the pros and cons and timing with your professional.

hazardous substances
Many older properties may contain hazardous materials such as

○ asbestos-based building materials
○ old paint on doors/windows etc containing high levels of lead
○ lead water pipes, especially hot water pipes.

Most of these won't be a problem until they are disturbed but then may pose a potential health risk to work people and to occupants. It is better to discover them at this initial stage when the professional can make appropriate recommendations.

detailed design

Once the briefing and survey stages have been completed, the design process begins. Depending on the job, things can then move very quickly. Various drawings will be produced, and amended as technical problems are encountered and solved.

It is important to show big furniture, such as beds or wardrobes, on the drawings in the design stage. People are sometimes reluctant to do this so early on, but without such knowledge, it may not be possible to position doors and services correctly.

For a new kitchen, a good idea is to 'practise' your way of working and needs: where are you going to use and store various electrical items? Where do you need sockets and taps? You should be quite clear on design and layout, even to the extent of having a cardboard mock-up made.

The professional might forget to discuss 'minor' items of the design with you such as the position of the radiators, power points etc, things that to you may be very important. So you should arrange meetings at regular intervals and work stages, and be sent plans, to ensure you are in agreement with the way the design is shaping up. Make sure you understand the drawings — better still, have the professional spell them out to you — including measurements so that you have a good idea of what any fittings, cupboards etc will look like.

If the design completed by the professional does not match up with your requirements, the professional may be reluctant to go 'back to the drawing board' even though it was his fault in misinterpreting your ideas. But once you have made your decisions, try not to make changes to your requirements. Every time you change your mind, you could run up a bill for abortive work by the professional.

You should be given some idea of the timing of the work, when it will start and finish, general indications of the sequence in which the work is to be done (although the actual timing will be in the hands of the contractor unless specifically instructed at the tendering stage).

You should ask for a meeting specifically to approve the final design before the professional moves on to the next stage.

contract documents

Once the design has been finalised, your professional adviser will start putting together the contract documents to be sent out to builders for quotations.

the documents

The contract documents of small projects generally consist of the following sections:

○ general preliminaries and conditions
○ materials and workmanship
○ prime cost sums and provisional sums
○ the works: specification and drawings.

general preliminaries and conditions

The general preliminaries deal with the conditions under which the work is to be carried out together with any special requirements that you might want to include. This section should describe the extent and purpose of the work, whether the property will remain occupied and any other factors that you and the professional think should be pointed out.

For instance, assume that you want a rear extension built on your house but there is no free access to the rear garden, only from the front. Also, your rather long front garden is full of prize-winning flowers and shrubs so you don't want any storage of materials or mixing of concrete in it. This will mean that the builder will have to do all this work outside your front gate. Not only will the workmen have a long way to carry materials but the builder will have to obtain special permissions from the highway authority to use the road or pavement. You also need to ensure that they won't make an awful mess and cause damage in taking all the debris and building materials through the house.

Any such requirements which will cause the builder more work will make the job more expensive. So, you should discuss with the professional what effect the conditions you would like to impose will have on the contract and the likely costs.

So that the builder can adhere to the conditions, and for them to be enforceable, they have to be reasonable. For instance, if you insert a condition that the workmen must wipe their feet every time they enter your property from outside, there are bound to be times when they forget and leave a few muddy marks on the carpet. The professional will be unable to do much about it. There is no effective sanction that he can take: it is too minor to 'end' the contract. When you 'phone the professional about this occurrence frequently, he will moan at the builder about it, who will almost certainly get very fed up. Unnecessary friction like this can harm relationships and start the contract down a very rocky path. Better to stipulate that the contractor puts down adequate dust sheets or thick polythene sheeting.

Some examples of reasonable conditions that have been inserted in contracts are given below. Maybe some of them could be adapted to suit your particular circumstance. Discuss these and any others with your professional adviser; you might jointly decide to miss some out or include more, depending on the circumstances.

examples of general conditions

"The working hours are to be 8am — 5pm on weekdays and 8am — 12.30pm on saturdays. No sunday working allowed."

"The working area is to be restricted to the following location:
. . . .
. . . ."
(insert description of area, but be realistic — the builder needs space to handle and work on materials)

"Remaining material storage and material preparation must be accommodated on the public highway immediately outside the customer's property or other agreed suitable location."

"Operatives are allowed to use the facilities of the kitchen, toilet and bathroom but are not allowed in the following areas:
. . . ."
(insert descriptions of rooms)

"Parking of the contractor's and operatives' vehicles must be done with due consideration for neighbouring owners and on no account block any of their driveways."

"Rubbish and debris are to be deposited directly into a skip or other suitable removal container and not deposited on the property. Rubbish is to be regularly damped down and covered with a tarpaulin to prevent dust from spreading."

"Where carpets, furniture etc are to be left in place, adequate clean dust sheets are to be provided at all times to prevent damage."

"The contractor is to ensure that all water services are reconnected by 5.30pm every evening and to ensure that the WC is usable and that there is at least a cold water supply to the kitchen sink."

"The contractor is to ensure that the building is left secure every evening. If windows and doors cannot be properly secured, temporary boarding is to be put in place."

"The occupants will be out for most of the working day and the contractor must have a named representative acceptable to the customer solely responsible for the security of the building."

materials and workmanship

This section sets the standard for the work by stating the materials to be used and how they are to be put together. This is an important section that will influence the cost, durability and quality of the work. Although its content will be technical, based on decisions by the professional, you should agree what level of quality is to be aimed at. Ordinary 'softwood' fixed together with standard nails, for instance, will cost less than hardwood and stainless steel screws but it probably won't last half as long. You should talk to the professional and try to balance cost with quality and durability.

prime cost (p.c.) sums

In small contracts, this section consists of sums of money that will form part of the total price, to cover items of work or the supply of materials that are not known at the time of preparation of the contract.

Prime cost sums are for work to be carried out by nominated sub-contractors or for materials to be supplied by nominated suppliers. One use of a p.c. sum is to cover work carried out by specialist sub-contractors where the actual cost of their work is not known. Examples would include an electrical contractor or timber treatment specialist.

If your bathroom is being refitted and you haven't quite made up your mind what type of bath suite you want, the professional may suggest that a prime cost sum is included in this section to cover these fittings. Once you have made your choice, the professional will instruct your builder to get those particular fittings and charge the cost against the appropriate p.c. sum.

Both you and the professional should be clear on the general type of fittings that will be chosen. If £300 is included for the cost of a 'standard' bath with average taps but you then choose a smart sunken number with gold plated pump action shower attachment costing £1200, the agreed contract sum will obviously be exceeded. It doesn't stop there. If you make a late choice and the builder was expecting a conventional bath, the plumbing and flooring may have to be changed, causing more expense. (Any late decisions may also lead to delays due to problems with delivery periods of suppliers.)

It is traditional in the building industry that the builder adds a percentage to p.c. sums to cover his overheads, profit and attendance. Overheads and profit depend on the policy of that particular builder. 'Attendance' relates to the amount of preparation and clearance work the builder will be involved in. For instance, most sub-contractors will expect the main builder to provide scaffolding, rubbish clearance, electricity, water. Timber treatment firms, for example, will want the floorboards lifting, and replacing once they have done the work. If the timber treatment firm charges £500 for spraying your roof timbers with preservative, the builder could add 10% for attendance with, say, 5% for his overheads and profit.

If your professional instructs the builder to buy a bath for £300, the builder is traditionally entitled to 2½% discount — whether or not the supplier actually gives it. The cost of a £300 bath, therefore, to you may be £300 + 2½% discount (not given by supplier) + 10% profit and attendance = £338.25.

provisional sums

Provisional sums are for work that cannot be fully described or specified at the time of the tender.

The professional may use provisional sums to cover an aspect of the work he has not yet sorted out, and is proposing to 'sort out on site'. An example would be forming a large opening in an existing wall. The professional may consider that it is not practicable at this stage to work out properly what sort of beam is needed over it, and that a provisional sum should be included to cover all eventualities. Unlike a p.c. sum, a provisional sum includes all profit elements.

The potential drawback is that the professional may not include enough money to cover the item. When the work has been done and the builder comes to put in his price for it, the cost may end up higher than the amount provided for that item in the tender document.

The best advice is to make all your choices before the tender documents are prepared and try to ensure that the professional has fully identified all the work so that the number of provisional sums is cut down to a minimum.

the works

The specification is a written document that describes the actual work to be done. (Some builders refer to it as a schedule.) It should be clear and precise and logically organised so that any builder can easily understand its meaning and content. It will be a technical document that will probably be difficult for you to check but you should read it very carefully to see if it does basically reflect the job you want carried out. That is why it is important to have briefed your professional adviser well, and to query anything you do not understand.

No two specifications are the same: different professionals adopt a different approach to their specification writing.

The document is usually divided into three columns by lines: generally, the far left hand column will be the reference of the specification clause, the actual clause typed out in the middle and the contractor's price for that item will be entered in the right hand column.

Drawings of the scheme to illustrate the specification also form part of the contract. The type and number of drawings will depend on the judgement of the professional but they should be clear enough to give an accurate indication of the type and extent of the work. Drawings may also have to be produced to obtain planning permission and building regulations approval.

the contract conditions

In most building schemes that involve a professional adviser acting on behalf of a building owner (the 'client'), a standard form of building contract is used. The most common type is produced by an organisation called the Joint Contracts Tribunal (the JCT). The JCT is made up of representatives from professional bodies, the building contracting industry and from local government organisations and the British Property Federation. The JCT has produced different types of contract to cover different types of scheme — from the small domestic job up to specialised multi-million pound schemes.

For schemes up to a value of £50,000 (at 1981 prices), the recommended contract is called 'Agreement for Minor Building Works'. (The current edition is March 1988 with a revised edition expected shortly.)

This is not the only option; your professional may recommend another type but should have a good reason. For example, a member of the Faculty of Architects and Surveyors might use one of their standard forms of contract — for 'minor works' or for 'small works' or for larger and more complex building works, as appropriate.

Agreement for Minor Building Works

Mentioned in the contract are

○ The Contractor — this is the builder who does the job.
○ The Employer — this is you (sometimes known as the building owner), the person who is paying the Contractor for the work.
○ The Architect/Contract Administrator — this is the professional engaged to design the work and make arrangements on your behalf with the Contractor who will carry out the work specified in the contract.

The following briefly reviews the main provisions of the JCT Agreement for Minor Building Works.

commencement and completion
The start and finish dates should be stated. Although the time should be kept as short as possible, a realistic period should be given. If too short a period is agreed, the contractor is more likely to over-run and cause contractual disputes. You must allow the builders to start on the commencement date. If you don't, they will not be bound by the completion date.

extensions of the contract period
If the work is not going to be completed within the contract

period through no fault of the contractor, the contract administrator (your professional) has to be informed as soon as possible in writing, with reasons, and give a new completion date.

non-completion
If the contractor has no good reason for not finishing on time, the employer can deduct 'damages' from the payment. The figure of damages is inserted in the contract as £xx per week or part thereof. It must be a realistic assessment of your loss; it is not a penalty clause.

completion date and defects liability
When the contract administrator is happy that the work is finished, he will issue a 'Certificate of Practical Completion'. This will signify the start of the defects liability period during which any faults are to be put right by the contractor at no extra cost. In the standard contract, this period is set at three months (six in Scotland) but can be altered to any period as agreed.

control of the works
Neither the contractor nor the employer can assign the contract to another party without the consent of the other.

sub-contracting
The contractor must not sub-contract all or any part of the work without the written consent of the contract administrator. This consent should not be withheld without good reason.

contractor's representative
The contractor must have a competent person in charge on the site at all reasonable times who is able to be instructed on behalf of the contractor by the contract administrator.

exclusion from the works
The contract administrator may issue instructions to order an operative off the site if there is a good reason to do so.

contract administrator's instructions
Your professional can issue written instructions which the contractor must comply with. If they are given orally on site, they must be confirmed in writing within two days. If the contractor doesn't carry out an instruction in a reasonable amount of time, the professional can issue a written notice pointing this out. If the contractor still doesn't comply, after 7 days the employer may bring in another person to do that item of work. The cost will be deducted from the payment to be made to the original contractor.

variations
Parts of the contract work may be omitted or added to by the contract administrator. This is done by written instructions ordering a variation. Variations should be priced in accordance with comparable prices contained within the contract, or the price should be agreed before the variation is carried out.

payment
Where the contract conditions are on a fixed price basis, as most domestic contracts are, the price is held firm throughout the contract (in Scotland, however, there is a 'fluctuations' clause option) and no additional payment can be claimed by the contractor for increase in costs except where these are imposed by the government (e.g. a new tax on pipes or a national insurance increase) or there is an agreed variation.

progress payments and retention
If requested by the contractor, the contract administrator will certify progress payments to the contractor at various stages.

A percentage deduction, called 'retention', will be made from each stage payment. It is usually set at 5% but this can be altered.

Whenever a 'certificate of payment' is presented to the employer, the money due must be paid to the contractor within 14 days. If it is not paid then, you are in breach of contract. Therefore, you must arrange your finances well in advance.

statutory obligations

The contractor must carry out the work in accordance with building regulations and all other statutory requirements, regulations and byelaws that relate to the works.

injury, damage and insurance

The contractor must take out insurance for any claim in respect of liability for personal injury to or death of any person or damage to property arising out of the works. If the contract is for new work (for example, a detached garage or shed), the contractor, and if the work is on an existing structure, the employer must take out insurance in joint names to cover damage (by fire etc) to the property and any materials on site for use during the course of the works.

Both the contractor and the employer shall provide to each other evidence of insurance, if requested.

determination

The employer may determine — that is, end — the employment of the contractor in specified circumstances. If the contract is properly ended, the contractor must leave the site and the employer is not bound to make any further payments.

The contractor, too, may end the contract in specified circumstances.

guarantee/warranty schemes

The JCT Agreement has a 'supplementary memorandum' to cover specific situations. Part E of this memorandum applies to work done under a guarantee/warranty scheme such as the Building Employers Confederation (BEC) guarantee scheme, and sets out how to adapt the Agreement for use with the scheme and what insurance shall be taken out, and stipulates that the defects liability period when the guarantee scheme applies shall be six months.

sub-contractors

Many contractors don't have enough people on their staff to do all the different types of building work required by some projects. For instance, when there is only a small amount of electrical work to be done on every job, it would not make sense to employ an electrician who would just sit around most of the time. Therefore, the builder will employ a separate firm of electrical contractors to do that aspect of the work as a sub-contractor. The main contractor is responsible for whatever work sub-contractors carry out, just as if his own employees had done it. You or your professional will not have an influence on the choice of sub-contractor. You can overcome this by providing a list of several sub-contractors from which the builder can choose, or by nominating a sub-contractor.

Where a contract administrator or an employer requests that a specific contractor is hired to carry out a specialist item of work, he becomes a 'nominated sub-contractor'. The JCT Agreement for Minor Building Works does not have provision for the nomination of sub-contractors. But you could provide for a nominated sub-contractor in the general preliminaries, so that his appointment will then form part of the contract.

An alternative is to use a different form of contract that provides for the use of a nominated sub-contractor. This would involve using a much more comprehensive contract that imposes many more duties and obligations on all involved than the complexity of the work would otherwise require. In Scotland, however, there is a set of sub-contract conditions for use with the scottish Minor Works Contract which is drafted to facilitate the use of bills of quantities and to permit the client to list the names of 3 or more sub-contractors who should carry out identified parts of the work.

the contractor and the sub-contractor

Most sub-contractors expect certain facilities to be provided by the main contractor such as scaffolding, plant, rubbish clearance, electricity, water, and preparing and making good. This is called 'attendance', and the builder adds on a percentage for attendance as well as for profit. In exchange, the main contractor takes on the responsibility and the hassle of co-ordinating the nominated sub-contractor's work.

Where you are arranging specialist work direct, your professional adviser should find out what facilities the sub-contractor you have chosen requires because the main contractor will have to be instructed to provide these. The contractor will have to be given as much notice as possible of the date the sub-contractor will be doing the work: if the sub-contractor turns up and everything isn't ready, he will go away without doing the work, charging for the waste of time. If the sub-contractor doesn't carry out the work on time, the main contractor's work may also be held up and he, too, will claim for unproductive time spent waiting around.

If these operations are not well co-ordinated, sorting out who was responsible for what problem will be very difficult.

insurance

Most home owners have two main types of insurance cover for their property:

○ buildings insurance (usually required by the body that provides your mortgage) — this covers the structure of the building in the event of fire, flood, storm, subsidence and other such insurable risks

○ contents insurance — this is optional and it is up to you whether you take out a policy. It covers possessions, furnishings and other property for specified risks, including burglary, fire, etc.

When building work is carried out on your home, the risk to your property increases in the eyes of most insurance companies. Insurance policies require the policyholder to take reasonable care of the property, and the builder will be under the same duty to his insurers. If, for example, he carelessly sets your house on fire, your insurers will pay your fire claim and then look to him, or his insurers, to repay their outlay.

If you are having your roof re-covered or work done to your walls, scaffolding might well be erected all around your property for several weeks. Whatever precautions are taken by the contractor, your home will be more vulnerable to break-ins both in terms of easy access to windows and that your neighbours are less likely to challenge strangers on the scaffolding on the assumption that they are the builder's employees.

If the windows are being replaced or you are having new openings formed in existing walls, the builder may well have to board these over temporarily for a few days. This will also make the place vulnerable.

Thefts from building sites are ever increasing. The mere fact of having a building team on your property will increase the 'interest' of the criminal community always on the look-out for lead, copper, tools etc.

The risk of accidental damage also increases during a building scheme, ranging from fire through to paint pots dropped on carpets. Most standard forms of contract for building work have a section relating to insurances that put responsibilities on both the builder and the customer. In the JCT's Agreement for Minor Building Works, it states that the employer (you) is responsible for taking out insurance in the joint names of yourself and the contractor for the existing structure of the house (including the contents) and for the works being done and the materials being used, to cover any damage or loss by the usual risks that a building insurance policy covers. It is standard practice for a householder to extend his buildings policy to cover the existing building, the new structure, materials and plant on site for the period of the contract.

It is important to reach a clear understanding with both the builder and the professional before the work begins on site to determine, and confirm in writing, who will be responsible for what. In most standard contracts, there is a requirement on both the builder and the employer to provide evidence of their respective insurance cover. A good builder will not mind producing his insurance policy for inspection. The employer should always tell his insurance company that work is about to start.

You should write (do not rely on a 'phone call) to your insurers or broker giving the following details

- a description of the extent of the works and the possible contract value
- whether any scaffolding or other temporary structure is to be erected
- when the work is due to start
- how long the work is expected to go on.

You should ask them whether your insurance cover will be affected. They may charge you an extra premium for any necessary extended cover or for deleting an imposed exclusion.

If your house has a burglar alarm system, be sure that no policy conditions are broken when, of necessity, the house is left without the alarm being set because the workmen are there. Check with your insurance company if your contents policy has specific requirements in regard to your alarm system and its operation.

As all of this could take several weeks, you should start the process off well in advance of the work starting.

obtaining a tender and choosing a builder

Once you have approved the scheme as developed by your professional and the contract documents are assembled, they will be sent by your professional adviser to building contractors for quotations. This is called 'putting the scheme out to tender'.

This is a very important stage. The builders who are to be included on the 'tender' list and asked to quote, should be properly vetted by the professional: any one of them could end up doing the job. The professional should be able to propose a number of builders and you also may know of a firm or two that it might be worth trying. For most small contracts, three or, at most, four builders will be sufficient.

Before you accept the professional's recommendations, you should ask:

○ what does the professional know about the builder?
○ have they worked together before and on what type of projects?
○ what sort of organisation? Is there an office that is attended all day or at least equipped with a telephone answering machine?
○ how many people does he employ? Does he employ operatives from all trades or does he put some jobs out to sub-contract? (The more work done by sub-contractors, the higher the chance of contractual problems through poor communication, co-ordination, control etc.)
○ is the builder a member of a recognised trade organisation? Does it provide a warranty or guarantee of work scheme?

BEC *guarantee*

If a builder is a member of the Building Employers Confederation, the work may come within the BEC Building Trust guarantee scheme. This scheme was originally established for work where the client did not engage a professional intermediary. A variant now covers small (up to £50,000) building work where an architect or other professional contract administrator has been appointed. Most general building and specialist work is included (not roof repairs unless part of other building work), provided it is carried out under the JCT Agreement for Minor Building Works with supplementary memorandum Part E. You pay £20 or 1% of the contract price (excluding VAT), whichever is the greater.

The scheme provides all-risks insurance for damage to the works or to goods or materials on site to be used on the work; an assurance that any structural defects for which the BEC member is responsible which appear during the two years following the six-months' defects liability period will be rectified; an undertaking that if the BEC member becomes insolvent at any time within the guarantee period, the contract will be completed or defects remedied by another BEC member. There is also a guarantee that if the BEC member fails to rectify defects or becomes insolvent, the scheme will meet any additional direct costs up to a set amount (currently £5000 plus VAT) incurred by having the work done by another builder, and also any additional fees if a professional has to act to ensure completion of the work.

All members of BEC are entitled to participate in the guarantee scheme (some are less willing than others but must not refuse to do so) and can provide you with literature and a copy of the scheme rules — look through these carefully to check whether your job would benefit from the scheme's protection.

If you want to take advantage of this scheme, you should tell the builder as soon as possible. He then arranges for the job to be registered. You have to complete a guarantee registration application together with the builder, preferably at the time of signing the JCT Agreement, and pay the fee then. You get a registration certificate from BEC within 7 days of your application.

At the end of the contract, the final certificates issued by your professional have to be sent to the BEC Trust so that they are alerted to their liability for any default that may develop within the guarantee period.

FMB *warranty*

If you and your professional have picked out a builder who is a member of the Federation of Master Builders and on their register of 'warranted' builders (a fairly select minority of FMB members), you can ask for your project to be carried out under the safeguard of their warranty scheme. This, too, is principally for schemes undertaken directly with a builder but — provided it has been negotiated with the builder before the work starts — can still apply if you have an architect or surveyor co-ordinating the scheme.

The warranty will ensure that for two years after completion of the work, defects through faulty materials can be reported to the Federation and, if agreed, will be rectified at no expense to you. Also, if the master builder becomes insolvent (or dies) before the job has been fully carried out and you take on another registered builder to complete the contract but this costs you more than the original contract price, the Federation will pay the difference up to a maximum of £8000. The warranty extends to the work of this second builder as he also is a 'warranted' member of the FMB. The cost of the warranty to you is 1% of the cost of the work (estimated by your professional and/or the builder), with a minimum fee of £5. You must use a standard form of contract, pay the premium (via the builder) and get the FMB registration certificate before the work starts.

is it worth it?

It would be worth asking your professional's opinion of the advantages of such a scheme for your particular project, in relation to the extra negotiations, paperwork and cost. He may feel confident with an established builder whose work he knows to be reliable without needing the support of paper protections.

references

All the builders included should be asked to provide the names of people they have done work for, who can be asked for a reference. Preferably, these should be householders like yourself. You should contact these people directly and ask questions along the following lines:

○ what was the standard of work like?
○ what was the builder's time-keeping like? Did the men turn up when they said they would?

○ were they tidy and considerate? did they take care when working in your house?
○ what was his paperwork like? did he confirm arrangements in writing? were his bills accurate and on time?
○ did they come back to put right any faulty work?

You should be careful how you interpret this feedback. In some cases, personalities may have been the cause of problems rather than failure of performance.

your choice

If you are not happy with the tender list, discuss the matter with the professional and put forward your suggestions. Remember, it is you who will be paying.

Be wary, however, of insisting that a particular builder of your choice is to be included on the list against your professional's advice. The success of any contract will depend on how well the builder and the professional work together. Many small builders, although they may have done minor jobs for you and your friends before, aren't geared up to be supervised by a professional. Any good builder should be familiar with the more formal, contractual approach to building work that a professional will be expecting. But you could ask your professional to find out whether the builder has worked with a similar professional in the past.

sending out the tender

Once a list of contractors has been decided upon, the professional should administer the tendering process in accordance with a professional code of practice for single stage selective tendering.

Once the tenders have been opened, the professional should check to see if they are all arithmetically correct. A tender report should then be prepared and sent to you, recommending which builder's price to accept. In most cases, this will be the lowest, but not always. If the lowest tender contains mistakes or inconsistencies, or the builder has questioned or qualified the contract conditions, or cannot meet your time-scale, the professional may recommend that you accept the second lowest instead. It may be possible for the professional to query the proposed cost of some of the component items and negotiate a reduction — the builder may have misunderstood what was required or the extent of it.

signing the contract

Before you sign the contract, the professional should organise a pre-contract meeting with you and the builder. As this person (and his workmen) will be working on your property for several weeks or months, it is important to meet each other as early as possible.

You should talk over the scheme to ensure that the builder realises what aspects are important to you. The sort of things you should confirm include

○ start and completion dates
○ the sequence of operations or the programme of the work i.e. when they are going to do the digging, concreting, roofing etc.
○ access to the dwelling, storage of materials, parking, use of facilities and any other requirements laid down in the preliminaries
○ insurances — make sure that it is quite clear who is supposed to take out which policy for what cover.

Be careful not to judge the builder too quickly. First impressions can be deceptive. Remember you want to buy the services of a builder who can competently carry out the works — you don't have to find him personally endearing, although that will help.

If the meeting shows that you and the builder will never manage to get on, it may be wiser not to offer him the contract, and to consider one of the other tenderers instead.

If you are satisfied, the professional will arrange for the signing of the contract agreed between you and the builder. The professional may offer to do the signing for you but you should do so yourself. Be very sure you understand exactly what is involved and what the terms of the contract mean before it is signed.

The contractor's responsibility is now to carry out the works as specified. The professional's role changes at this stage, from that of a personal consultant acting in your interest solely to that of the 'contract administrator'; he has a duty to stand as an arbiter between the parties in cases of dispute. You, as client, may see this change and think the professional is taking sides with the builder; in fact, he must administer the contract fairly for both parties.

the role of the professional when work is in progress

Once the work begins, the professional will assume the role laid down in the contract conditions. He will take it as his duty to act impartially between you and the builder. He will see you and the builder as a couple of players where the contract conditions are the rules of the game and he is the referee.

For instance, if the contractor carries out work that is sub-standard, the professional will instruct that the work be done again, at no extra cost to you. Conversely, if you are unhappy about some part of the work but the professional disagrees and considers it adequate, you may be overruled and the builder instructed to carry on. In this way, many decisions will be a matter of the professional's judgement and may from time to time be questioned by the other party.

on site

The professional should inspect the progress of the work in accordance with the agreement between you and him. This normally imposes a duty to make occasional visits to see if the work is being carried out in accordance with the builder's contract. The professional does not give whole-time supervision: he will make adequate visits to the site at critical times — for example, to check foundations.

It is the builder's right to organise the work in whatever method he sees as suitable. The professional has no power to tell the builder how to execute the work on a day-to-day basis. For example, if the contract period has been set at 10 weeks, it doesn't matter if the builder is only doing work for 3 to 4 days a week: so long as the work is progressing steadily and is finished within the contract period, it is up to him.

You will certainly be 'on site' more than the professional is, especially if you are living there. You will watch the work develop day by day and will naturally have great interest in it. You must resist the urge to get involved directly or interfere. If you are not careful, you could jump to unjustified conclusions. For instance, the uneven and unacceptable plasterwork may actually be the first coat only, waiting for its final coat next week. The door frame that they have recently put up may appear too rough — but the builder was going to smooth down before decoration, anyway.

Too many queries too often put will begin to undermine the trust between all parties. If there is something that is obviously a worry, contact the professional discreetly and ask what his opinion is. If you are concerned about the work the contractor is doing, never instruct the contractor directly; only the professional should do that. But you should let the professional know of your concern and ask him to take the appropriate action. Avoid, in particular, asking the builder for anything to be done differently or anything extra to be done — you have to go through the professional for that. Otherwise, it is impossible for the professional to keep track of costs.

You should request regular meetings on site with the professional and the contractor to discuss progress. These should be at 2 to 3 week intervals, depending on the length of the contract.

rises in costs

Once the work has started, changes in the scope of the work are likely to arise. Even the best prepared schemes cannot allow for unknown factors. The foundations may have to be dug deeper, dry rot may be discovered where it wasn't expected — all part of the rich tapestry of the building process.

The costs of variations and additional work sometimes balance out with savings in other work so the final price may be about the same as the original contract price. This is an optimistic view. Many contracts, especially those on older buildings, are very prone to overspending.

Where the professional gives verbal instructions on site for changes or additional work, these must be confirmed in writing by issuing 'variation orders' or 'architect's instructions' or 'contract instructions', and producing revised drawings.

As soon as possible after the professional informs the builder of these changes, an instruction should be issued.

variation instructions

These instructions are usually filled in on standard forms printed by the professional institutions. A typical instruction should contain the following information:

○ the name and address of the professional's practice
○ the name and address of the employer
○ the name and address of the site and the contractor
○ the date the instruction was issued and the reference number of the instruction.

The main body of the instruction consists generally of

○ the written instruction itself
○ two small columns to the right, one headed 'omit' and the other 'add'. These are cash columns and usually have 'total' boxes at their base.

All instructions should be signed by the professional. There are usually several copies of the instruction produced, one for the contractor, one for yourself (insist on one if you don't get it) and for the professional's own office requirements.

A SIMPLE EXAMPLE

Imagine that your contract involves general repair of your property including eradication of dry rot and the installation of a new bathroom. The work started three weeks ago and there have been a number of changes to the contract:

○ the dry rot has spread further than anyone had expected and affected more of the ground floor timbers than allowed for in the contract
○ you've changed your mind about the new front door: rather than the expensive hardwood type you now want a cheaper softwood version
○ you've now decided on the bathroom fittings you want and have passed the list on to the professional

○ because the costs are rising, you want to miss out the redecoration of the windows. (You've decided to do them yourself.)

Initially the cash columns will probably be left empty as the cost of many of these items will be subject to further discussion between the professional and the builder. If this is left for some time without anyone giving you an idea of how the contract price is changing, you could be in for a big surprise at the end of the job. You should stipulate that the professional gives you a 'best' estimate of the changes every time an instruction is issued and regular updates (say, monthly) of the anticipated final cost.

Each variation or instruction will either 'add' to the contract sum or reduce ('omit') it. In the above example,

○ the dry rot work will add to the contract: the cost should be entered in the 'add' column of the instruction
○ the new softwood door should be cheaper than the one originally included and so it should reduce the amount of the contract: reduction in cost entered into the 'omit' column
○ in the original documents, a 'prime cost' sum should have been included to cover the cost of bathroom fittings. The comparison of that amount and what the chosen fittings actually cost will determine whether it adds to or reduces the contract amount
○ the omission of the window painting will reduce the contract amount.

The extra costs or savings brought about by variations will be summarised in the final account and the appropriate adjustment made to arrive at the final contract sum (as shown on page 75).

problems with variations

If any of the instructions appear confusing to you, phone the professional and ask for an explanation. This is one way of keeping an eye on what's going on.

In many cases, the professional won't inform you of extra work until after the instruction has been given to the contractor, committing you to paying for it. This is because

○ it was a small item of work that will balance out against the savings
○ it was an urgent item of work that had to be done as soon as possible (e.g. water leak, gas leak etc)
○ the progress of the work must not be held up.

If the professional had to get back to you for every extra item and wait for your approval, the contract would almost certainly be held up. This could lead to extra claims from the contractor for wasted working time.

To prevent problems like this, before work starts you should set up a procedure with the professional to deal with extra costs. For instance, it is advisable to have a 'contingency' amount, a percentage of the total contract price (say, 5% or even 10%), to meet the cost of variations. You should stipulate that you are told if extra works threaten to push the cost above this level. You can then discuss whether money can be saved in other areas to bring the costs within your limits again.

You should also ask the reason for the extra works. Were they reasonably unforeseen extras or did the professional forget to put these items in the original contract documents? The latter may point to a possible liability on the part of the professional.

FINAL ACCOUNT

Employer:	J. Jones 2 Anywhere Street NEWTOWN
Architect:	P + P Architects 22 Market Street NEWTOWN
Contractor:	ACME Construction Unit 1A Industrial Estate NEWTOWN

Summary of Architect's Instructions

	OMIT	ADD
Architect's Instruction No. 1	6 223.06	–
" " No. 2	–	3545.01
" " No. 3	–	2421.07
" " No. 4	–	401.12
	6 223.06	6367.20
Total Adjustment		+ 144.14

Original contract sum	15 847.92
plus adjustment	144.14
Final contract sum	15 992.06

Summary of payments

Certificate at payment No. 1	5186.48
No. 2	4625.03
No. 3	5780.75
No. 4	399.80 (Final)
	15 992.06

Contract period: 16 weeks

Contract start: 7 February
Contract completion: 30 May

Extension of time: none

I/we have studied the above information and agree that it
is a true representation of the final contract position.

Signed   *Aebert C. Mead* ....(Contractor)
       6ᵗʰ December 1988. (Date)
.... *Phal Pallm* .... (Architect)
    9-12-88 ..... (Date)

satisfied with the work?

For the duration of the contract, it is the professional's responsibility, in his role of contract administrator, to ensure that the quality of the work meets the required standards.

When the contractor considers that the job is complete, your professional will be notified and a 'snagging' meeting organised. This is where the work is thoroughly inspected and a list given to the contractor of defects and omissions that must be put right before the contract can be declared completed. You may be invited to this snagging meeting to give your opinion of the work. Or your professional may invite you to a pre-snagging meeting to give your opinion of the work prior to his meeting with the contractor. (His reason for this is that meetings with client and contractor present can degenerate into squabbles; it is easier for the professional to explain to the client that he is being unreasonable on a particular point if the contractor is not present.) Although the technical standard will be a matter of the professional's judgement, you should make your opinions known.

Once the snags have been rectified to the satisfaction of the professional, he will issue the 'practical completion' certificate. All the outstanding and sub-standard items should be identified and finished before the practical completion certificate is issued. This marks the beginning of the defects liability period. At this point the contractor will end operations on site, and return only if any defects are reported.

the defects liability period

For most standard types of contract, this liability period is set at three months from the date the certificate of practical completion is issued, but it can be agreed for it to last for six months (or longer). This is separate from any product guarantees you may get: for example, for central heating or damp proof course work.

Any defects in the work that become apparent must be put right by the builder at no cost to you and within a reasonable time. Normal shrinkage and cracking, unless due to incorrect materials or workmanship, are not included. You should always report any defects to the professional in the first instance. Never call out the builder on your own judgement: if you do and the defect is not the responsibility of the builder, you'll get presented with a bill for the builder's time.

The response time of the builder will depend on the nature of the defect. A roof leak or a broken pipe will obviously require swift attention while a crack in the plaster could wait for a time. In fact, for any defects of the non-urgent, cosmetic variety, the professional may suggest that they wait until the end of the defects period when they all can be done together.

As the end of the defects period approaches, the professional should organise a joint inspection with the builder to check for any defects. Before this meeting, you should let the professional have a list of any defects you think the builder should put right. The professional will make a list after the inspection meeting and give it to the builder, who should do the remedial work within a reasonable time, usually two weeks.

Once the builder thinks that all is complete, another inspection will be held and, if the work has been done, the job will be finally signed off when a certificate called the 'making good defects' is issued. This releases to the builder all the money retained from interim payments and so is a very important stage.

dissatisfied?
If the professional is prepared to issue a certificate despite

there being work you are not happy with, you must be careful how you act. Once the certificate is issued, you must pay the contractor. If you don't, the contractor will be able to take legal action against you. If the professional is accepting work you think he should not, that is a dispute with him and not, in the first instance, with the contractor.

payments

In most building contracts, it is normal to pay contractors by instalments, usually at four-weekly intervals. Where the project is relatively small and the contract period short (say, six weeks), the contractor and the professional may suggest just two payments, possibly one half way through the contract and the balance when the work is finished.

Whatever the agreement, it is the professional's responsibility to assess the amount and value of the work completed at that time and 'certify' the amount that the contractor should be paid. This is usually called an interim payment or progress payment. The professional will issue to you and the builder a standard form of 'interim certificate' that states how much the builder is contractually due. The value of a certificate is made up of the following:

○ the value of the work completed
○ the value of any extra work
○ the value of any materials that are on site intended eventually for your job.

An interim certificate usually includes the following information:

○ the name and address of the builder (contractor)

Architect's name * and address:	P+P Architects 22 Market Street, NEWTOWN	**Interim certificate**

Employer's name J.Jones
and address: 2 Anywhere Street,
NEWTOWN

Serial No:

Issue date: 11·2·88
Valuation date: 7·2·88
Instalment No: 2
Job reference: P+P/J.J/04

Contractor's name ACME CONSTRUCTION
and address: Unit 1a, Industrial Estate
NEWTOWN

① I/We certify that in accordance with
Clause 30 of the Standard Form of Building Contract, 1963 Edition,

under the Contract

dated: 21·1·88   in the sum of £   15   847·92

for the Works: NEW REAR EXTENSION

situate at: 2 ANYWHERE STREET, NEWTOWN

interim payment as detailed below is due from the Employer to the Contractor

Total value. . . . . £ 10 327·90
*includes the value of works by nominated sub-contractors as detailed on
direction form no.   dated*

Less retention . . . . £   516·39
*after deducting any retentions released previously or herewith
(as detailed on the attached statement of retention ②)*

Balance (cumulative total amount certified for payment) . . . . £ 9 811·51

Less cumulative total amount previously certified for payment . . . . . . £ 5 186·48

Amount due for payment on this certificate . . . . £ 4 625·03

(in words) Four thousand, six hundred and
twenty five pounds and three pence only

All the above amounts are exclusive of VAT

Signed _____ Architect *

Contractor's provisional assessment of total of amounts included in above
certificate on which VAT will be chargeable £   "   %

This is not a Tax Invoice

Notes: ① Where the form of contract is the Agreement for Minor Building Works 1968, delete this line and insert
'Clause 10 of the Agreement for Minor Building Works first issued 1968'
② Delete words in parentheses if not applicable.
③ This form may be used for the purposes of releasing retention on practical completion, on partial possession
or on making good defects. When used for this purpose and no statement of retention is issued, insert here
appropriate wording from the following:
'including release on practical completion/partial possession/making good defects'.

© RIBA Publications Ltd. 1977

○ the name and address of the employer (you)
○ the name and address of the professional (contract administrator)
○ the reference number of that certificate
○ the date on which the professional carried out the valuation
○ the date the certificate is actually issued.

The main body of the certificate should include the original
contract sum and the date the contract was signed.

The first figure given is the 'gross' value of all the work that
has been done so far.

The second figure is the retention amount. This is a sum of
money, as specified in the contract (usually 5%), held back
from the contractor as a sort of 'insurance' for the client. The
retention is money that is eventually due to the contractor. But
if the builder were to go bankrupt or refuse to finish the work,
you could hold on to this retention money and use it towards
employing another builder to complete the work.

The third figure is the gross value minus the amount of the
retention. This is the net value of the work done up to the date
of that certificate. The fourth figure is the net amount of money
paid to the builder on the last certificate i.e. last time's gross
value minus the retention then. This amount is deducted from
the net value of this certificate and the resulting figure is the
amount now due to be paid.

VAT is due on interim payments where applicable; the builder
may invoice you for this separately.

You will be contractually bound to pay the amount on the
certificate within 14 days of the date on the certificate or of the
builder invoicing you for it (whichever the contract stipulates).
It is advisable to check the amounts of interim valuations. If
you are unhappy about the figures, you should discuss the
matter with the professional as soon as possible, but you are
not entitled to withhold payment beyond the 14 days — that
would be a breach of contract.

The professional has a duty not to over-value the work that has been completed. If he does this and the builders leave the site, they would have been paid for work that they haven't done.

For the same reason, the professional should not include in the valuation the cost of any defective work. For example, if a brick wall has been built very badly and the professional is asking for it to be knocked down and rebuilt, no money should be paid for the wall until it has been completed properly.

penultimate certificate
This is the last-but-one interim certificate. It is issued when the job has been finished and the 'practical completion' certificate has been issued. The method of calculating this payment is the same as the interim certificates but the retention amount is less for the duration of the defects liability period. If the normal retention was set at 5%, then it will probably reduce to $2\frac{1}{2}$%.

final account
Once the defects period has finished, the builder and the professional get together to draw up a 'final account': a statement of the final cost of the contract. Although there has been no work done over the last months, this final certificate may well include a fair amount of money.

The contractor must submit to the professional documented details of payments due to him.

The professional should produce a final statement of contract cost that has been adjusted to accommodate all the changes that occurred while the job was being done. If the costs of any changes were not fully discussed and agreed when the extra work occurred, you may have to pay a lot more now for work that was done quite a time ago.

An additional payment could be due to a builder because the contract period has been extended through no fault of the builder. Many builders price a job according to how long the contract period is, apart from the cost of actually doing the work. This is because there are certain fixed costs that relate to time: the cost of transport, office overheads and even the foreman's salary might be apportioned over the contract period. For example, if the project involved re-roofing of a house that the builder expected to take 4 weeks, and the contract period is extended, the builder could be in a position to make an additional claim for loss and expense incurred.

A typical final account should include

- ○ the original contract price
- ○ the original contract period
- ○ a list of all the variation instructions issued and their effect on the contract price
- ○ a revised contract price
- ○ details of any extensions of time granted and the revised contract period
- ○ a summary of all payments made
- ○ the total now due, including the retention money.

The main function of the final certificate is to release the remaining retention money which formally ends the contract.

You should make sure that the retention money you have held on to all this time is available to pay to the builder at the proper time. You should remember that although in your possession, it is the builder's money, so don't spend it on something else (e.g. a holiday). You have 14 days in which to pay.

value added tax

All costs of the work will be subject to VAT at the standard rate (at present, 15%) if the builder is registered for VAT. The builder will normally bill you for the cost of the work and VAT together, but may submit separate invoices, one for the work, one for VAT.

keeping control — a summary

You should try to set up a monitoring system that strikes a balance between interfering and keeping your finger on the pulse of the scheme. The aim is to spot anything that is going wrong at an early stage so that adjustments can be made before things get out of hand. Despite this, you should always try and create an atmosphere of trust between yourself, the professional and builder.

You should seek to agree a programme of meetings/information exchange at key points in the scheme's life.

1. Briefing meeting — to discuss with the professional your requirements; written note of discussion to be kept.
2. Survey meeting — to show the professional around your property and point out relevant features, give information etc.
3. Design (draft) meeting — to see design drawings and discuss any amendments before the professional produces finished version; discuss the cost and budget at this stage.
4. Detailed design (final) meeting — to see the finished version of the drawings and other relevant documents before they go out to tender; agree cost and total budget, revised as necessary.
5. Pre-tender meeting — to discuss tender list of contractors and procedure for tendering; ask for your own complete set of tender documents.
6. After the tendering — to receive tender report from the professional with recommendations, including a copy of the priced tender documents.
7. Post-tender meeting — to decide with the professional which builder to choose and to confirm contract conditions; get any queries clarified now.
8. Pre-contract meeting — with the chosen builder and the

professional to sign the contract and discuss and plan the works.

The following work-in-progress meetings/information exchange should be a minimum:

○ site meetings between professional, builder and you — will depend on the length of the contract but one every two to three weeks should be sufficient; a proper written record of these meetings should be kept, copies to all parties
○ variation instructions — you should receive a copy of all instructions issued for variation of contract, with a best estimate of the cost implication
○ interim payments — along with each certificate, the professional should include a financial statement of the current state of the cost and whether the contract cost will be exceeded or the ending will be delayed
○ snagging meeting — you should get advance notification of this meeting between professional and builder to inspect the work, for you and the professional to produce a snagging list (copy to you)
○ final snagging meeting — to inspect remedied work
○ practical completion certificate issued — start of defects liability period
○ defects liability inspection by the professional with builder — advance notice of this inspection to you and a copy of defects notified to the builder
○ end of defects liability period — final inspection by professional of remedied work
○ final certificate — the certificate and statement of final account: outstanding payment required in full.

when things go wrong — with the contractor

One of the advantages of employing a professional to organise the scheme is that he will use the provisions of the contract to ensure that the work is completed satisfactorily. Even if there are a few temporary setbacks — sharp words or formal exchanges of letters between the professional and the builder pointing out respective obligations under the contract — the project should not suffer from such incidents. But sometimes more serious problems occur, relationships break down and the builder either pulls off site or is removed from the scheme.

The professional should advise you on appropriate action to take in the particular circumstances. If you have subscribed to the BEC Building Trust guarantee scheme or the Federation of Master Builders' warranty scheme and your contractor's failure to perform falls within its protection, you or your professional adviser should at once contact the relevant body, give details of what has gone wrong and ask for the scheme to be invoked.

action by the employer (you)

A limited number of situations are specified in the JCT contract when you can end ('determine') the contract:

- o if the contractor without reasonable cause fails to proceed diligently with the works or wholly suspends the carrying out of the works before completion
- o if the contractor becomes insolvent or bankrupt.

If this happens, the contractor must give up possession of the site and the employer will not be bound to make any further payments.

If the work is completed by another contractor and the cost then exceeds the original contract price, the original builder should be required to pay the difference provided that the work carried out by the second builder exactly matches that described in the original contract.

It is imperative that at this stage professional advice is sought and adhered to. It may even be necessary to appoint a quantity surveyor to assess the value of the work done and materials on site. At this point, scale fees go out of the window and costs escalate. Depending on the amount of work done by the first contractor, the professional would be involved in a lot of additional work, for which you will have to pay

○ a survey of the work completed and preparation of revised contract documents for the completion works
○ the organisation of the tendering process to get a competitive price for the completion works
○ additional administrative work in sorting out the amount owed to or by the original contractor when the completion works have been finished.

If the final cost of the completion works far exceeds the orginal contract sum, you may have to go through the courts to recover this from the original builder. This will involve more time spent by the professional in supplying your solicitor with the necessary information for a court action.

Such action against contractors is sometimes met by a counter-claim alleging some breach of the contract by either the professional or the client. This puts the case firmly in the hands of the legal professionals and represents the point where many individuals withdraw from the action as the legal costs soon dwarf the contested amount.

Where the JCT Agreement was used and disputes arise with

the contractor and cannot be resolved, the standard conditions allow for the matter to be referred to arbitration. An arbitrator, generally appointed by the professional organisation, considers both sides of the argument and comes to a view that the parties must accept. Arbitration precludes taking court action later.

There is a new law, however, the Consumer Arbitration Agreements Act 1988, which says that even if there is a clause in the contract making arbitration compulsory as a means of resolving disputes, arbitration cannot be imposed without the consumer's written consent.

action by the contractor

The contractor can determine the contract, giving 7 days' notice, if the employer

○ fails to make progress payments on time
○ interferes with or obstructs the execution of the work
○ does not make the premises available
○ suspends the carrying out of the work for a continuous period of one month or more
○ becomes bankrupt or insolvent.

other problems

There are other areas where disputes or disagreements may occur.

not finishing on time
A completion date will have been set down in the contract and agreed by the contractor. If there is good reason for delay, the professional will issue an 'extension of time' certificate. This should state the reasons for the extension, such as

○ additional works have occurred so there was more work to do than first thought
○ the weather was unusually bad when external work was being carried out such as roofing, concreting etc. But this bad weather has to be worse than normal for that time of year. For instance, if the builder gives a price for re-roofing in winter, he should have anticipated a certain percentage of the time to be spent waiting for better weather
○ if any sub-contractors or suppliers that you had wanted to use deliver late or hold the works up.

For the householder, a delay of a few weeks may not be so bad, almost expected, but the issue of an extension-of-time certificate has financial implications. The contractor may well submit a claim for additional expense and loss, to cover general overheads such as a proportion of the cost of the firm's offices, sometimes the cost of the foreman etc. These costs are apportioned on a time basis to each of their jobs. So, if longer time has to be spent on any one job, such a claim, provided that it is reasonable, will have to be paid.

If the contract period is going to be extended, you should ask the professional to find out if an expense and loss claim will be made by the builder. If one is, it should be fully itemised and entered on the final account and incorporated in the revised contract sum.

If the contractor does not finish the work in time and cannot blame anyone else, the professional may recommend to you that 'damages' should be deducted from the payments to the contractor. Damages must have been specified in the contract. They have to relate to real loss and not just a penalty for being late. For instance, if your elderly and frail grandparent was staying in a hotel and the pets were in kennels while the work was going on and they have to stay there longer than anticipated, this cost could be claimed as real loss and so be deducted from the payment to the contractor. Only the amounts for circumstances stated in the contract can be deducted.

not putting defects right

If defects occur within the defects liability period and the original contractor does not show any interest in coming back to put them right, the professional may advise that you can employ another contractor to do the work and take the cost from the retention money held back during the defects period. You should keep the original contractor advised, in writing, that this course of action has been adopted; your professional may well do this for you.

later defects

Once the work has been completed, the defects period has come to an end and the final account has been settled, you may be forgiven for thinking the whole thing has at last finished. In some cases, this will not be so.

Defects may become apparent after a longish time: cracks may appear in brick walls, the roof of your extension may start to leak, the new guttering may begin to sag. These problems (referred to as 'latent defects') may be the fault of

○ the builder for not constructing the building properly or not in accordance with the specification or drawings, or
○ the professional for designing or specifying inadequately or not inspecting the work properly.

In some instances, there may be a joint responsibility for latent defects. If in later years, you discover what were latent defects on your property, write to the professional who organised the work, describe the alleged defect and request a report from him. If you feel that you are not getting a satisfactory answer, see your solicitor for preliminary advice.

when things go wrong — with the professional

A professional will administer the contract using his 'best judgement'. There may be times when you don't agree with this — what happens then? You may find yourself halfway through a contract in dispute with a person you employed to protect your interests. If you understand a few basic rules, however, such a situation need not harm the contract too much, if at all.

relationship between professional and client

Most of the professional institutions suggest that the central plank in the relationship between the client and the professional is one of trust. If the professional is the right person for you, a good working relationship should be able to survive a few knocks. If you begin to doubt the advice of the professional and don't sort it out quickly, the success of the whole venture will be threatened.

Do not let things drift on. As soon as something happens that you feel is not right, take action. First of all, contact the professional and tell him what is worrying you. Try to resolve the matter informally. Describe the problem and your growing doubt in his ability; sometimes it can be a simple misunderstanding.

If you get no satisfaction, tell the professional that you are not happy and that you intend to refer the matter to the head of the professional's firm. You should state your opinions calmly and succinctly, referring to any correspondence and incidents as necessary. Be clear about what action you would like taken. If this gives you no joy, there are a few remedies that are offered by the professional institutions.

If the professional is practising on his own or is himself the head of the firm, you'll have to consider appealing to the professional institution direct.

getting a second opinion

You could ask the professional whether a second opinion would be useful (the cost of this will have to be borne by you in addition to the fees for the first professional). The RIAS warns that clients should be wary of getting informal second opinions from friends within the building industry who may not have all relevant knowledge. It is possible to get a second opinion without the knowledge of the appointed professional; the second appointee may, however, be unwilling to offer advice without informing the first. If the originally appointed professional discovers that you have gone behind his back to another one, the position of trust will be further eroded.

help from the professional institutions

The professional institutions have codes of conduct that their members have to abide by. If the professional you have employed belongs to one, contact the secretary of the institution and ask for details about that code of conduct. You may find that this covers only serious misconduct (e.g. fraud), not a breakdown in trust, incompetence or negligence.

The Professional Practice Department of the Royal Institution of Chartered Surveyors (RICS) investigates complaints against chartered surveyors that relate to

○ unjustifiable delay in dealing with your affairs
○ failure to reply to your letters
○ disclosure of confidential information

○ failure to disclose conflicts between your interests and the private interests of the surveyor
○ dishonesty.

If a member is found to have breached one of the rules, the RICS can reprimand, severely reprimand, suspend or expel him from membership.

The Professional Conduct Committee of the Royal Institute of British Architects (RIBA) can take up complaints that relate to

○ dishonesty or lack of integrity
○ improper conduct of a client's affairs or inadequate liaison with a client
○ abuse of confidentiality or lack of discretion
○ allowing other interests to conflict with those of the client
○ improperly obtaining commissions.

The Royal Incorporation of Architects in Scotland (RIAS) is prepared to entertain complaints of

○ disgraceful conduct
○ conflict of interest
○ failure to have client's approval
○ failure to adhere to budget
○ failure to observe procedures laid down in the conditions of appointment.

about fees
Legally, you are obliged to pay the fee agreed at the outset between you and the professional. If no fee had been agreed, the fee charged must be a reasonable sum. A criterion of reasonableness could be the scale of recommended fees issued for the guidance of members by some of the professional institutions.

The RIBA and RIAS standard conditions of appointment state that any difference or dispute arising on the fees charged may, by agreement between the parties, be referred to the RIBA or RIAS, for an opinion provided that

○ the member's appointment is based on the RIBA/RIAS *Architect's appointment* and has been agreed and confirmed in writing; and
○ the opinion is sought on a joint statement of undisputed facts; and
○ the parties undertake to accept the opinion as final and binding upon them.

This service is free, and relatively speedy. Any dispute which cannot be resolved through this procedure can be referred to arbitration.

arbitration

Your first action should be to consult the commissioning agreement between yourself and the professional to see whether a dispute resolution procedure is built-in (i.e. arbitration). The standard contract of many organisations includes an arbitration clause. The procedure is generally based on The Chartered Institute of Arbitrators' standard consumer arbitration scheme. The rules of the scheme (and of specific schemes for which the standard rules have been adapted) provide for an inexpensive and relatively informal method of resolving disputes. No legal costs are awarded. The procedure is not designed to deal with disputes in which, in the opinion of the arbitrator, issues are unusually complicated and would need a hearing and oral evidence to be resolved properly. Generally, the arbitrator will decide disputes by reference to written submissions and documentary evidence only.

The Royal Institution of Chartered Surveyors offers a chartered surveyors' arbitration scheme also which is run independently by The Chartered Institute of Arbitrators for the resolution of disputes between RICS members and clients. (The scheme, which started in June 1988, at present operates only in England and Wales; a similar scheme may be set up in Scotland.) The rules of the scheme, explanatory notes and an application form are available from the professional practice department at RICS and from the Chartered Institute of Arbitrators.

The scheme is limited to disputes which

○ arise between chartered surveyors and their clients (not third parties)
○ involve a claim for compensation on the basis of an allegation that the chartered surveyor is legally liable to the client for breach of professional duty
○ involve issues basically suitable for arbitration on documents only, without a hearing or oral evidence. (An inspection of the property can be included in the scheme if the arbitrator so decides.)

Each party pays a registration fee (currently £57.50 inclusive of VAT). Either party may be ordered by the arbitrator to reimburse the other's registration fee.

As with all formal arbitration schemes, both sides are bound by the arbitrator's decision and award. You cannot subsequently sue the surveyor about the same matter in court.

points to ponder
Appealing to a professional institution as a method of resolving a dispute has a number of drawbacks. In all cases, going to the institution or taking legal action will put the 'nail in the coffin' and destroy any remaining trust between you and the professional. This may be counter-productive.

Most disputes require quick action. For instance, if you think the professional is not inspecting the work properly or is certifying payment for work that you think is below standard, you will want the matter resolved quickly. Complaints made to professional bodies take weeks to investigate. For most smaller building schemes, this will be a long time after the scheme is completed.

Professional institutions exist mainly to promote the activities and protect the interests of their members. A few members acting unreasonably will spoil the image of the rest so the institutions are prepared to bring these members into line. Even if the institution finds against its own member, the sanction — reprimand, suspend or expel from membership — will be designed to deal with the member's conduct rather than resolve your dispute or compensate you.

But the very act of taking your complaint through this process may encourage the professional involved to take your comments a bit more seriously and try to resolve the complaint before it goes any further. If it establishes responsibility for the alleged act or omission, it might strengthen your resolve to pursue it through legal channels. It is rare for an institution to comment in such a way that it could be called on as an 'expert witness' (but it may be able to advise on the nomination of a suitably qualified person).

taking legal action

How or when to take legal action will vary depending on the circumstances. Before taking any legal action, you should get some initial advice from a solicitor, choosing one who is experienced in building contract disputes. (The local reference library may have a copy of The Law Society's regional directory in which solicitors state what expertise they claim to have.)

Because professionals are so aware of the increase in legal actions being taken against them, most have professional indemnity insurance to protect them against such claims. (This is, of course, in your own interest: if there has been a design error, for example, it is better to be able to claim against a properly insured professional than to have to claim and prove negligence against someone whose only assets are likely to be house and car.)

One of the conditions that these insurance policies set down is that when there is any mention of an action being taken against the insured professional, the case is handed over to the insurance company to handle straightaway.

If you as much as mention legal action, delays will occur because the professional must notify the insurers, and may perhaps have to stop work on the job in the meantime.

If you proceed, you will probably find that you or your legal representative will be approached with the offer of an out-of-court settlement for an amount less than your claim. Depending on the strength of your case, your legal representative may suggest you accept even though the sum offered does not cover all your financial loss. Just because you think that you are 'right' does not mean that you will be successful in court.

Employing a builder on your own

This chapter looks at employing a builder direct where

- you are not employing a professional at all or
- you employ a professional for only part of the scheme leaving yourself to organise the rest.

The advice relates to all types of work. Whether it's a jobbing builder repairing a leaking gutter or a larger firm putting up a two storey extension, the common factor is preparation.

As long as you spend time familiarising yourself with the issues involved, you will have a good chance of organising a successful project. Without a professional acting on your behalf, you will be more vulnerable to the bad practices of some of the construction industry. If your approach is methodical and well planned, you should be able to redress the balance in your favour.

some preliminaries

The success of employing a builder yourself without the help of a professional will depend on how well you communicate your requirements to the builder and how good he is at carrying them out.

If you want to organise repairs on your property, you will have to decide what the cause of the problem is. This is not always simple: rising dampness can be confused with condensation, roof leaks mistaken for plumbing leaks, cracks appear without an obvious cause.

If you are the average lay person with only a basic knowledge of buildings and their repair, you will have to familiarise yourself with technical matters. You don't need to become an expert or attend bricklaying nightclasses — just get acquainted with the sort of work the builder may need to carry out. Here are a few ways of doing this.

○ Talk to friends or family who have some knowledge of building construction or have had similar work done in the past. But beware of the DIY 'experts'. Although they are well meaning and may have completed several impressive jobs themselves, their advice may not be appropriate for your situation.

○ Buy an up-to-date DIY or domestic maintenance book that is comprehensive and relatively detailed. The cost of even an expensive £25 book could be repaid many times over by problems avoided — cheaper still if you can borrow it from the library. Make sure that it is the most recent edition. Don't rely on some old DIY book your uncle bought you six birthdays ago: building technology may have moved on considerably.

If you are going to commission new work, an extension perhaps, or a reconstruction or conversion, get as much information as you can about possibilities by visiting a building centre. If you want to 'gen' up on the technicalities and developments in the construction world, you could refer to the government-funded Building Research Establishment which claims to be "the major source of independent and authoritative information for the construction industry in the UK". The BRE produces a range of publications for professionals in the construction industry, including illustrated leaflets, detailed reports and books, information packages, digests of current building technology (varying prices, minimum order £3). A list of current publications is available from Publication Sales, Building Research Establishment, Bucknalls Lane, Garston, Watford WD2 7JR.

employing a professional for part of the work

Consider employing a professional to prepare part of the project. For instance, if you want a small and simple extension to your house, you may need technical drawings done so that building regulations approval and/or planning permission can be applied for. If properly done, these will also provide the builder with enough information to quote for and carry out the scheme.

Assume that you want to build a single storey side extension to your house. You'll probably need a design for the extension in terms of its appearance and how it is to be constructed. The drawings should include enough written constructional information to act as a type of a specification. For this you will need to employ a professional. Once someone has drawn up the scheme, you may feel you can handle getting estimates and supervising the work on site yourself.

A chartered quantity surveyor, particularly in the regions, could be asked to prepare a specification for your project, provide some costings and then identify one or two builders in the area known to him as performing well. You could then supervise the work. The cost saving of this approach as against having a professional throughout could be quite significant.

Given the importance of getting the specification right, a quantity surveyor preparing the specification and contract for you would give you the confidence that the specification is complete and also that it is written in a manner that a builder is used to.

partial services

An appointment on the basis of 'partial services' is allowed for by most of the professional institutions. The fee can be negotiated either on a time basis or as a lump sum, or be on a percentage basis. Where an architect is commissioned under the RIBA's *Architect's appointment*, which splits the architect's basic services into different stages, his interim payments are based on the progressive stages of work. For partial services only, the payment may be a reduced percentage fee based on the architect's estimation of the total cost.

By employing a professional for only part of the job, future liability for any defects may be compromised and difficult to prove. If your building did develop faults that you suspect are due to design inadequacies, the professional could be protected by the fact that he did not inspect the work 'on site', and so avoid liability.

Some aspects of the design produced by the professional may not be clear to the builder, who will turn to you for further instruction. It is essential that you go through any drawings, plans and specification with the professional very carefully and ask that anything you do not understand be explained to you in terms that you can grasp and communicate to others. This is important also so as to be able later on to check that the builder is following the plans/specification.

asking the builder

Some building firms offer design expertise as part of their service to people for whom they are going to do work.

Many established builders have a great deal of experience in the repair and maintenance of existing buildings and are usually willing to offer advice on how best to solve a problem.

Before you take the advice of any one builder, get the opinions of a couple of others. Ask them to come to look at the house, and discuss with you how to achieve what you want and what needs to be done and to give you a rough estimate of the cost. You may find that none of them agrees and you'll end up with three different approaches. In this case, you should balance each proposal against the research you have carried out and choose the one which appears most logical to you.

Assume that the old cast iron guttering around your house is leaking in several places and you want to get it repaired. You ask three builders verbally to "Repair my guttering". The quotes for the job could vary dramatically from very expensive to relatively cheap.

○ Builder no. 1 looked at the guttering and saw most of it was in a very poor condition. He knew that that particular type of guttering was no longer made so he wouldn't be able to replace the defective lengths only. His price therefore included complete replacement of the whole guttering system in cast iron. This builder put in the highest price.

○ Builder no. 2, also seeing that the whole guttering would have to be replaced, priced a complete new system but in PVC which is cheaper than cast iron. He submitted the second lowest price.

○ Builder no. 3 thought that he could replace the leaking sections only, with PVC lengths. Where the old cast iron sections and new PVC meet, he would make it watertight by sealing with 'mastic'. His was the lowest estimate of the three (but the repair would last for only a short period, possibly a matter of days).

Always bear in mind that the builder has a vested interest in the outcome of his advice. Either he may simplify the matter to get you to appoint him and then come back to you with the real complications — and, of course, the extra costs. Or he may over-complicate a simple job in order to increase the value of the work.

specifying the work

To be able to obtain accurate and competitive prices from several builders, you should produce a written document or specification. The specification part of a building contract describes in words the work required.

Details relating to finishes, such as tiling, plastering, flooring, decorations, and other specialist requirements such as joinery, electrical requisites, bathroom and kitchen fittings, will need to be given.

Your 'specification' should provide the necessary information for the builder to estimate a cost. This is especially important when you are asking several builders to quote because unless they are quoting for similar work, comparison of their prices will be misleading.

If a lay person cannot draw up a specification, he should state what is required simply — and request the contractor to specify what will be done (e.g. depth of hardcore, its quality etc). Remember that even if no specification is drawn up, in law the materials and workmanship have to be of a reasonable standard.

the 'reasonable builder'

By the same legal principle, if someone puts himself forward as a builder (or any other man of skill), he will be judged as such. He will be expected to produce work of a standard common to the construction industry. The test of reasonableness is: what could a person expect from the average, reasonable builder?

This means that your specification doesn't have to include everything involved in that building operation. It should indicate its nature and extent. For instance, you ask a builder to "Fit a new glazed door in the back door frame."

A reasonable builder should include for

— taking off the old door and disposing of it
— providing a new door of the correct dimensions hung on proper hinges
— buying and fitting the glass
— possibly refitting the original lock and handle.

A reasonable builder might claim that the price did not include for

— providing anything but the cheapest softwood door (this might not be as secure or as durable as you would have wanted)
— what size of glazed opening (a new door with one large glazed panel is cheaper for the builder to fit — but all the other doors and windows in the house have numerous small window panes)
— what type of glass (the builder might fit clear glass when you wanted patterned glass)
— painting the new door (the builder should leave the door with a 'priming' coat on but might claim that you didn't ask for it to be painted)
— any new locks (if your old door had old and insecure locks on it, you'll get them fitted back on to the new door).

This example shows that even a reasonable builder could leave you disappointed with the end result without actually doing anything unreasonable.

A more suitable description of this work would be: "Take off old door and fit new hardwood varnished door on new hinges, new lock and handle. Door to have small glass panes with patterned glass to match other windows of house."

(Nowadays, fitting a new glazed door is more likely to be done by a specialist firm, such as a member of the Glass and Glazing Federation, than by a builder.)

official standards

For just about every building operation there is a defined standard. The British Standards Institution (BSI), the national standards organisation, publishes

○ British Standards — standards relating mainly to materials, their type and quality. Most building materials and components should have a 'BS' number.
○ Codes of Practice — describing how the various materials should be put together to produce finished work of good quality.

These are very technical documents but you should be aware of their existence and what they cover. Copies should be available at central reference libraries.

Manufacturers who choose to make their product to a British Standard will probably quote the BS number on the pack or label. Manufacturers of certain types of goods may also show the 'kitemark'. This is the BSI's registered certification trademark which indicates that the BSI has issued a licence to the manufacturer, after independent tests have been carried out to ensure that the product complies with the BS and that the firm's quality system complies with the international quality standard.

Your builder may suggest using a particular new product or material that has an Agrément certificate. The British Board of Agrément (BBA) is a government-sponsored organisation principally concerned with the testing, assessment and certification of innovative products, materials, systems and techniques for the construction industry, to encourage and ensure their safe and effective use. The BBA issues certificates to products that reach the required standards of performance.

An Agrément certificate is a published document (£2.50 each). The certificate includes the Board's opinion of the fitness for specified purposes of the particular product and the context in which it is to be used and how it should perform.

The manufacturers of products awarded an Agrément certificate are subject to quality control surveillance by the BBA or its agents during the period of validity of the certificate. The BBA symbol should be on or attached to a certificated product; if not, ask the supplier or builder whether it has an Agrément certificate and what the number is.

The BBA publishes a directory of approved installers and an index of current Agrément certificates listed in alphabetical order and by name of product/manufacturer and by use category. These publications cost £1 each from the British Board of Agrément, PO Box 195, Bucknalls Lane, Garston, Watford, Herts WD2 7NG.

permission to do the work

Building work is subject to a variety of statutory controls. When planning a building project, you have to be aware at an early stage of all the permissions you may need. Many will have to be applied for weeks or months in advance of the actual work starting and may affect the design and layout of your scheme and the method of construction itself. You should take all of these requirements very seriously. You may be tempted to try and 'get away with it' but this could have frustrating consequences:

○ if your neighbours object and inform the authorities, you could be made to take down the work at your own expense and, in some cases, be fined for breaking regulations
○ if you sell the house, the potential purchaser could well discover that you have carried out work without permission. The sale could then easily grind to a halt or fall through.

The main permissions that are usually required for small domestic projects are dealt with below.

planning permission

If the project you are planning substantially changes the external appearance of your property or constitutes 'development' as defined under the Town and Country Planning Acts, you will have to make a planning application to the local planning authority, to get permission to carry out that work.

There are certain types of work, called 'permitted development', which do not need planning permission. Generally, this includes work which is maintenance, improvement or other alterations which affect only the inside of the property. The sort of schemes that you may be able to carry out under present legislation include

○ if the house has not already got an extension, you can build one provided it cannot be seen from the front of the house and it is below a certain cubic capacity or volume
○ you can build a porch to the front of the property provided

it is less than 2 sq metres in area, less than 3 metres high and no closer than 2 metres to the front boundary
○ a garden shed or greenhouse, maximum height 3 metres and not bigger than half the size of your garden
○ fences, gates or walls to the front can be built provided they are below 1 metre high; to the rear you can build up to a height of 2 metres.

What would need permission includes, for example, a front or side extension, or one to the rear that is bigger than the permitted development limit, a 'change of use' of a building (e.g. converting a house into two flats or turning an old barn into a dwelling).

Planning Aid for Londoners has published a *Householder's Guide to Planning Permission* (£1 from the London branch of the Royal Town Planning Institute).

The Department of the Environment and the Welsh Office publish a free booklet *Planning permission: a guide for householders* which includes information about work that does not need planning permission (i.e. 'permitted development'), and also *Planning appeals* which is a guide to the procedure you can follow after a refusal. Both booklets should be available at council offices and citizens advice bureaux.

Telephone or visit the planning department of the local authority to discuss your ideas with a planning officer there. Most are very helpful and should give you clear advice on whether you need to make an application or not. If you do, they will probably give you an indication of what would, or would not, be acceptable.

If planning permission is required, you will have to fill out the proper forms, submit drawings and pay the necessary fee to the local authority. (The fee for an application for "the enlargement, improvement or other alteration" of an existing dwellinghouse is currently £33.) If the scheme is at all complex, you will almost certainly have to engage a professional to produce the drawings, as they will have to show accurately the extent and type of the work you propose. Most lay people unskilled in this area would find this very difficult to do.

Planning approvals can take a very long time, especially if there is an objection by a neighbour. Obtaining planning permission can take as long as six months, even for straight-forward schemes, so plan well in advance.

planning permission in Scotland

In Scotland, similar procedures are laid down in separate town and country planning legislation. Under permitted development categories, the percentage by which a house (other than a terrace house) can be extended without needing permission is 20% of the original size up to a maximum of 115 cubic metres. An extension to be built over 4 metres high and within 2 metres of the boundary, or which would occupy more than 50% of the curtilage, requires planning permission.

An applicant is encouraged to discuss a proposed application informally with the planning authority at an early stage in order to clarify the information needed and action to be taken. For instance, a notice of the application must be served on neighbours, telling them where plans and drawings may be inspected. When an application has been made and the requisite fee paid (£27 for alteration to an existing dwelling), the planning authority must give the applicant notice of the decision within two months, or such longer period as may be agreed with the applicant in writing.

listed buildings

Under the town and country planning legislation, the Department of the Environment lists buildings that are of special architectural or historic interest. Any building that has been 'listed' cannot be demolished, extended or altered in any way that affects its character, both exterior and interior, without obtaining 'listed building consent' from the local authority. This requirement is in addition to planning permission. There are grades of listed buildings, and the strictures on what will or will not be allowed to be done vary with each.

If your home is listed as being of architectural or historic interest, or is in a conservation area, you should consult the planning department straightaway and/or take professional advice. The employment of a professional is almost essential for almost all types and size of work if the pitfalls of the legislation surrounding such buildings are to be avoided.

You can find out whether your property is listed from the planning department of the local authority. If it is, you must proceed with care. This is because you have to get permission to carry out work that would be permitted on non-listed buildings — for instance, front porch, rear extension. Depending on the property and its features, the local planning authority could have an influence on the guttering and rainwater pipes that you fit, or even on the colour of paint you use.

If you carry out work on a listed building without consent, the council can serve an enforcement notice on you that will require you to put the building back into the condition it was before the work was carried out.

If your home is in a designated conservation area, there will be restrictions on what you can do to the exterior without obtaining permission — check with the local planning department.

Useful leaflets issued by the Royal Town Planning Institute include *Your planning application, Should I appeal? Where to find planning advice (regional)* and *What is listed building consent?* (this includes information on conservation areas and tree preservation orders).

listed buildings in Scotland

In Scotland, too, there are mandatory lists of buildings of special architectural or historic interest, in three categories. You can find out whether your property is listed by contacting the planning department of the local authority. Lists may also be inspected at the Historic Buildings and Monuments Directorate at 20 Brandon Street, Edinburgh and at the Royal Commission on the Ancient and Historical Monuments of Scotland at 52-54 Melville Street, Edinburgh.

Any building that has been listed cannot be altered, extended or demolished without obtaining listed building consent from the planning authority. The procedure is similar to that for obtaining planning permission.

If you carry out work which is not approved, the planning authority may serve an enforcement notice on you, requiring the restoration of the building to its former state.

If your home is unlisted but lies within a designated conservation area, no demolition can take place unless conservation area consent (similar to listed building consent) is first obtained.

trees

If a tree is too close to the walls of an extension you want to build, it may threaten the stability of the whole structure. In some cases, a tree may be right in the way of the extension or garage you want to build.

Before you rush out with an axe, you should check with the local authority planning department whether the tree is protected by a tree preservation order under the planning legislation. You will be fined if you do not first get permission to cut or lop any tree that is under a preservation order or is in a conservation area.

superior landlord

If you own the leasehold of your property in England or Wales, someone else will own the freehold, probably the person or company you pay your ground rent to. In most cases, if you are planning to carry out only repair and maintenance works, you do not need to tell your 'superior' landlord but the work may be the landlord's responsibility, not yours: check your lease carefully.

Improvements, however, do need the consent of the landlord. Also, some leases have such odd covenants and clauses in them that even the most basic work might theoretically breach the terms of your lease.

The term 'freehold' has no meaning in Scots law. There may be restrictions in the original feu charter (about subdividing your home, for example). The owner of property in Scotland should consult title deeds to ensure that the proposed work does not contravene these. The deeds may indicate that certain permissions are required from feudal superiors.

Ask your solicitor or the person who holds the lease what relevant restrictions there are. The document may be so complex that employing a legal professional's advice on this one point may be worth considering. If you do carry out work prohibited by the lease or its schedules, the landlord could terminate your lease. In any case, the infringement could be picked up when you try to sell the place, and cause frustrating delays.

If your house is mortgaged to a building society or bank, there may be a clause in your mortgage deed under which you must inform the mortgagees and/or get permission before carrying out major changes to the property.

building regulations

The Building Regulations (1985) govern how buildings are to be constructed, and all building works have to conform to them. The regulations are administered by the building control department of your local authority, from whom building regulations approval has to be obtained.

A copy of the Building Regulations can be consulted in local authority offices or in most public reference libraries, but a lay person would need guidance to interpret them. The Building Regulations also include a section called 'Approved Documents'. These are meant to give practical guidance on how the requirements can be met; they, too, will probably be too complicated for the average lay person. There is a Department of the Environment explanatory memorandum *The manual to the Building Regulations 1985,* published by HMSO (£6.20).

There are two ways of obtaining building regulations approval:

○ *full plans:* you have to submit a full set of drawings before the work starts. If these meet the requirements, they will be approved by the local authority.
○ *building notice:* you give notice to the council in a written form that you intend to carry out the work. No approval is formally given but the work is inspected 'on site' to ensure that it complies with the regulations. The risk with this method is that you could find that the building control inspector asks for work to be done in excess of what you had planned. At least with the full plans approval method, you know what to expect.

With both methods, a fee is payable that varies with the cost of the project. In the case of full plans approval, you will be applying in advance of builders' quotations, so you will have to assess the cost of the scheme for the fee. For extensions, garages, and loft conversions, the fee does not vary according to the cost of the project: fixed charges are payable.

The fee is generally payable in two stages. For *full plans* applications, the first fee is payable when the application is made and the second is payable after the first inspection of work has been carried out. For *building notice* applications, a composite fee, equivalent to the first and second fees above, is payable after the first inspection. It is usual council policy to invoice for these fees after the work starts.

It is an offence to

○ fail to submit a full plans application or building notice
○ build in a manner that contravenes the Building Regulations (work may have to be opened up for inspection or even pulled down)
○ fail to give notice to the local authority at certain stages of the work.

Work can be varied from the original plans but what is done must conform to the regulations.

It is your responsibility to get building regulations approval. Building control officers are usually very helpful and will give you good advice. The building control officer may warn you that changes to what you propose will be required which could cost a lot of money. You should obtain building regulations approval before you approach builders for quotations. You should apply as soon as possible — it can take a few weeks for the application to be processed.

For most schemes, it is likely that you would have to employ a professional to prepare the application and plans for you.

Although the Building Regulations apply to the whole of England and Wales, each local authority may interpret them slightly differently. Many building control departments are short of staff and so have taken policy decisions to limit their involvement. For instance, they may limit their inspections on all projects to just foundations and drains. As long as you have made proper application to the local authority for building regulations approval, whether they inspect the work or not should not rebound on you: it is their responsibility to ensure that work is checked properly.

Once your scheme gets building regulations approval, the local authority should send you an official form that states any conditions or further requirements. They should also attach 'Building Regulations inspection cards'. These are notification forms that should be sent to the local authority's building control department when the work reaches certain stages so that a building control officer can come to inspect the work to check that it is up to the proper standards.

When you have appointed a builder, you should hand the cards over to him and make the builder responsible for sending these to the building control department at the right moments.

Building regulations approval and planning permission are two quite separate requirements and getting one is no substitute for the other.

building control in Scotland

Scotland has its own building control system and regulations. Before building starts, you must ensure that a building warrant is obtained from the local building control authority, who will advise on what drawings and other information will be required to enable them to check for compliance with the regulations. Only very limited plans may be necessary in the case of certain minor works. A fee is payable according to the estimated cost of the project. A warrant is also required for the demolition of a building.

The local building control authority is the district or islands council or regional council, from whom the standard application form (containing notes for the guidance of the applicant) and table of fees can be obtained. A warrant is valid for work starting within 3 years (at present) of its issue.

The local authority must be notified when building work begins and subsequently at specified stages (for example, when drains are ready for testing). During construction, the work may be inspected by building control staff, and other tests may be required to establish compliance with the regulations.

Before the new part of the building may be occupied, it is necessary to obtain from the local authority a completion certificate. This provides formal confirmation that the building has been erected in accordance with the warrant and with the building standards regulations.

In exceptional cases, there are arrangements to permit relaxation from requirements of the regulations; the local authority can advise on how to apply for an individual relaxation. Reasons for relaxation can include, for example, unreasonable difficulties posed in alteration work.

As in England and Wales, a building warrant applies only to approval of the standard of construction and does not absolve the owner from the need to get planning permission, where applicable.

Proposed revisions to the building standards legislation in Scotland aim to simplify the building control requirements — for example, by allowing for self-certification and 'class' warrants.

the specification

Your specification will obviously be very different from the one a professional might produce, but so long as you follow some basic rules, the end result should be sufficient for its purpose.

The specification (also known as 'schedule') should be a simple and straightforward document consisting of concise sentences that describe the works in a logical order. Don't try to use unfamiliar 'technical' terms.

The layout should be clear. It would be useful to have the following features:

○ the first page should start with your name and address (plus telephone number/s)
○ each page should be clearly numbered
○ each separate job should be indexed in some way by either letter or number so that you can refer to it clearly
○ each page should include a 'cash' column on the right hand side so that the builder can easily insert a price against each 'clause'. If the description of all the jobs takes up several pages, these cash columns should be carried forward so that a running total can be kept
○ at the end of all the pages, a 'total' box should be provided and enough space for the builder to enter his name, address, signature and date of the quote. (Remember that VAT will be additional.)

Don't try to be too clever. Don't try and write down anything you do not understand or can't explain to a builder. You'll look pretty daft if the builder catches you out. They will respect you much more if you have simply stated your requirements, leaving the technical stuff to them.

what you want done

If you have a number of jobs you want doing, they should be split into 'external' and 'internal'. Some people start at the top of the house or room and work down. For example:

OUTSIDE	INTERNAL
chimney	ceiling
roof	walls
gutters	windows
walls	doors
windows	floors
doors	services (plumbing,
paths/fences	electrics etc)
drainage	

This is not an exhaustive list: whatever method you adopt, you should stick to it to make sure that you don't miss out anything.

You should define the extent of the work. For instance, if you want part of your concrete path dug up and replaced, you should describe how much of it. This could be in words or measured area:

"Re-concrete the front drive from the front gate back to the large tree on the left"

or

"Re-concrete 10 metres of the front drive from the edge of the boundary"

This would also apply to other things such as repointing brickwork, replacing guttering, replastering walls. The builder will then be clear on how much work is required.

Always be specific about the location on the house. If you ask the builder to "fix the leaking gutter", he may find another smaller leak somewhere else on the guttering and not repair the one you wanted. A better description would be:

"Repair leaking gutter to rear of house approximately over the position of the patio doors to the lounge."

It may seem long winded but it's the best way to be accurate. To be on the safe side, you could add: "Check the rest of the guttering and specify where repairs are necessary, and estimate for them."

the quality of the work

The choice of materials or components to be used has an effect on the cost and the quality of the finished work, in terms of durability and appearance.

Before you instruct the builder, you should investigate the alternatives available for that particular job. If it's something like a door or a gutter, a trip down to the local DIY store will be useful. You should consider

○ whether you like the appearance
○ what sort of quality/durability you want
○ what price you think you can afford.

If you have decided, make a note of who makes the product, name, address and phone number if possible and, more importantly, the reference number of that particular product. When you come to write your 'specification', you will be able to define precisely the components you want, to ensure that the quotes you get are directly comparable.

If you specify cheap materials, the builder may not want to use any that are of poor quality, and would not take on liability for your meanness. If he does not like what you are specifying, he can propose alternatives and state the reason. If no specification is given and the choice of materials is left to the builder, they must be of a reasonable standard.

Make sure that you have written everything down. A builder will only quote for what he is asked to. If you cannot decide on an item to be supplied (for example, what shower fitting), say "Allow a sum of £250 to be adjusted to actual cost of shower selected". This would be a 'prime cost' (p.c.) sum.

contract conditions

When you are employing a builder on your own, whether for a small maintenance job or something more substantial, you should have a written agreement even if the work is straightforward and the relationship with the builder informal. The aim is to protect your interests should a dispute occur.

A standard contract for building work that can be used as a checklist of items to agree with the builder has been devised by the consumer protection division of the Environmental Services Department of Birmingham City Council and by the Consumer and Environmental Services Department of Barnsley City Council.

a form of contract

The following sections outline a list of clauses that could be incorporated into a contract document that you are sending out for quotations. The word 'employer' refers to you, and the word 'contractor' to the builder plus the other tradesmen whose work he controls and co-ordinates.

Employer/customer: . . . .
(your name, address, telephone number/s)
Location of job: . . . .
(if not as above)
Contractor/builder: . . . .

1. THE WORK TO BE DONE
The contractor will carry out and complete the work as outlined in the attached specification/drawings in a good and workmanlike manner in accordance with all relevant British Standards and Codes of Practice, all for the sum of   £ . . . .
Reference of documents attached: . . . .
. . . .
. . . .

(If you have any drawings, quotes or other related information that the builder will need in order to produce a quote or do the work, you should give them references and note these down here. This will make them part of the contract documents.)

2. The contractor will provide all the labour, plant, materials and equipment necessary to complete the work.

3. The work to start on . . . .
The work to be completed by . . . .
(Put in the dates if these are essential to you; otherwise, leave them for the builder to fill in.)

All work must proceed regularly and diligently.

The completion date will be extended only if the contractor is prevented from completing the works by factors outside his control. The contractor must notify the employer in writing of the reasons for any delay as soon as they are known and state the new completion date.

If the contractor, without good reason, fails to finish the work on time, the employer will deduct from any outstanding payments due to the contractor damages which represent actual loss to the employer, as set out below:

. . . .
. . . .
. . . .
(These should be items of expenditure, on a weekly basis, that would be caused by the work not being finished e.g. hotel charges if you can't live in the house, furniture in storage etc)

4. The contractor must remove all rubbish as it accumulates and all

tools, surplus materials etc from the site and leave it in a clean and tidy condition within 14 days of the completion of the contract.

5. The value of any variation of the work should be agreed before that work is carried out. Only variations properly authorised by the employer will be paid for.

6. The contractor will comply with all statutory requirements, local and national regulations and bylaws that relate to the work. The contractor will make all notifications, arrange inspections etc in connection with the works.

7. If the employer insists on the use of specified methods or materials that, in the opinion of the contractor, are not suited to the use that they are required for, the contractor will not be liable for any loss or damage resulting, provided that it is not due to the negligence of the contractor.

8. The contractor will not use any sub-contractors on the scheme without the express written approval of the employer.

9. The contractor shall take out insurance to indemnify the employer against any liability, expense, loss claims or proceedings in respect of

○ personal injury or death to any person
○ any injury or damage to any property

arising out of or by reason of carrying out the work. The contractor is to ensure that any sub-contractor also takes out similar insurances. The contractor shall provide a copy of his insurance document and send it to the employer.

10. The employer shall take out insurance for loss or damage due to normal insurable risks to

○ the existing structure and contents owned by the employer
○ the works, all unfixed materials and goods intended for the works, placed on or adjacent to the site (except plant tools and equipment owned or hired by the contractor).

The employer shall provide evidence of this insurance, if requested.

11. Once the contract is completed, the builder will submit a final

account to the employer, adjusted to take into account any variations. This will be paid within 14 days by the employer.

12. Where the period of the work is more than one month, staged payments will be made.
(These will be usually at one month intervals but can be varied by agreement of the parties.)

13. The employer may deduct 5% of the total of staged payments as retention. At completion, this amount will be reduced to 2½% for the duration of the defects liability period.

14. The defects liability period will be for 6 months. Any defects that arise during this period due to faulty workmanship or materials, will be put right by the contractor at no extra cost. Written notice of these defects must be sent to the contractor before the end of the defects period.

15. Once the defects liability period has ended and all defects put right, the employer will release the remaining retention money.

16. The builder must provide all facilities required under the Health and Safety at Work etc Act 1974 and include it in the price.
(These facilities, such as proper scaffolding, good ladders, toilet facilities etc, are the responsibility of the contractor to provide.)

points to ponder

Not all of these clauses need be included. If you are replacing a few roof tiles, most of these clauses won't apply. In fact, if you give such a document to a jobbing builder, he'll probably run a mile. In some cases, you may be well rid of him — he may be the cowboy you didn't want.

The whole purpose of drawing up a set of 'contract documents' is to control the building project. If a builder gets upset and does not want to get involved because of the formality, it may be because he finds paperwork a chore that he would rather not do (his job is building work not secretarial). Some may find it threatening but some simply find it an insult to their integrity to put things in writing.

Some builders who are competent and trustworthy may not consider such a contract applicable to the amount and type of work you want done. Imposing a lot of conditions will bring a 'cost' to a contract that may be out of all proportion to the control and protection you really need. These 'costs' are difficult to define but are nonetheless real. For instance

○ on receiving a specification with conditions attached, some builders may assume that these conditions will cause them additional work in either organising or carrying out the work, and so include in the quotation a higher overhead cost
○ if you specify a defects period and retention, this will mean that the builder will have to do without part of the payment for the duration of the defects period and, where defects do occur, the builder will have to return to put them right. Again, some builders may increase their overhead rates to account for this possible extra time.

conditions for small works

If you want only a limited amount of work done, the following clauses may be more relevant for your needs, with fewer conditions expressly imposed on the builder.

1. The builder will carry out and complete the work as outlined in the attached specification/drawings in a good and workmanlike manner in accordance with all relevant British Standards and Codes of Practice, all for the sum of   £ . . . .
Reference of documents attached: . . . .
                   . . . .
                   . . . .

2. The builder will provide all the labour, plant, materials and equipment necessary to complete the work.

3. The builder must remove all rubbish as it accumulates and all tools, surplus materials etc from the site and leave it in a clean and tidy condition within 14 days of completion of the contract.

4. The builder will comply with all statutory requirements, local and national regulations and bylaws that relate to the work. The builder will make all notifications, arrange inspections etc in connection with the works.

5. If the employer insists on the use of specified methods or materials that, in the opinion of the builder, are not suited to the use that they are required for, the builder will not be liable for any loss or damage resulting provided that it is not due to the negligence of the builder.

6. The builder shall take out all necessary insurances.

7. Once the contract is completed, the builder will submit a final account to the employer, adjusted to take into account any variations. This will be paid within 14 days by the employer.

8. The defects liability period will last for 3 months. Any defects that arise during this period due to faulty workmanship or materials, will be put right by the builder at no extra cost.

If a builder is concerned about the sort of conditions you've imposed, discuss them to see if there is a sensible compromise. It would be a shame if you were to lose a good builder just because of a few copied-out clauses from this book!

The builder may present you with a contract drawn up by his trade association. For example, the Federation of Master Builders has a 'small works contract' for its members to use; the Building Employers Confederation has one linked to the BEC guarantee scheme. If you have decided to use a builder who offers to work under a guarantee or warranty scheme drawn up by his trade association, you may have no choice but to use the standard terms of contract and will not be able to add your own conditions. Similarly, many specialist firms have their own agreement or contract and may refuse to accept any conditions you propose.

Choosing the builder

If you do not know of any builders, you can ask the Building Employers Confederation (in Scotland, the Scottish Building Employers Federation) or the Federation of Master Builders for a list of members in your area. Membership of these organisations is restricted to builders with a certain standard of competence.

Before you include a builder on your list, you should find out more about him (as you would do even with a professional adviser). Look out for builders working locally and watch how they are progressing, what equipment they are using and how they are working.

The size of a building firm will affect the structure and decision-making process of the firm. Many of the differences may be academic but the one of central concern is — control. Who makes the decisions? Who gives the orders? You will not want to waste time with someone who can't take action when required, and if things begin to go wrong, you'll need to know who to complain to.

Small firms — could be a one person business (usually the owner) or the owner and just a few other employees. The owner usually 'works' on the site a lot but disappears occasionally to visit other clients, do office work etc. Many work from home, office not staffed all day, telephone message-taking machine, wife/relation as accountant/office worker/dogsbody. When they have a lot of work on, they usually call in sub-contracted tradespeople to help them out, most probably other small firms.

Medium sized firms — probably a company with two or three directors with an employed work force able to undertake most general building jobs, tackling larger and more numerous contracts. The directors, although still involved with the jobs in progress, spend time setting up other deals and attending to the needs of business. They probably employ a foreman or a charge hand on each job to run the work on site. Depending on the structure of the firm, the foreman may have delegated authority over a number of issues but refer major decisions or disputes to the directors who will probably have an office with a part-time/full-time secretary and perhaps other staff.

Larger firms — not exactly Barratts or Wimpeys but firms with a large annual turnover carrying out large contracts for councils and other bodies, and also for individual private clients. The directors/owners will almost certainly spend most of their time on business matters. A contracts manager is sometimes employed to ensure that all the different jobs are running smoothly. Most sites will have a foreman/charge hand looking after that particular job. This type of firm will have a much more sophisticated office structure. Many of the larger building firms have small jobs divisions which are experienced in the type of work generally described in this book. Many large or well established firms have their own work/quality estimators — that is, surveyors who check that the craftsmen have carried out the work as detailed in the contract to the level of the contract price.

builders' qualifications

You may find a builder with the initials MCIOB after his name and/or who calls himself a 'chartered builder'. This indicates full membership of The Chartered Institute of Building (CIOB). There are various grades of membership of the CIOB, depending on the examinations that have been taken and the age and experience of the particular builder, from student to fellow (FCIOB).

A candidate for full membership, in addition to passing examinations in building technology and construction and management, quantity surveying and estimating and building law, has to undergo an interview by a panel, appointed by the Institute, to ascertain, among other aspects of his ability, that he can apply theoretical knowledge to problems "in the . . . field of building experience", that he displays "the capacity to accept professional responsibility and the leadership/management qualities expected", and that he has "the ability to communicate."

One of the objects of the Institute is the "establishment and maintenance of appropriate standards of competence and conduct of those engaged, or about to engage, in the science and practice of building". So, if you are disappointed with the performance of a builder who is a member of the CIOB, you should refer to the Institute to invoke their rules of professional conduct, which require members "to discharge their duties to an employer or client with fidelity and probity".

trade organisations

The building industry has formed trade organisations who set standards of performance that their members have to conform to. Over recent years, these trade associations have extended their role by offering the public 'guarantee schemes' that attempt to ensure that work is satisfactorily completed even where the original builder becomes insolvent or just disappears.

Guarantee or warranty schemes are particularly effective where a builder goes bankrupt or dies. In this situation, you would be unlikely to get any money because you would have to join the long line of creditors, nor likely to get the work finished. With the guarantee/warranty schemes, you get some useful cover in this situation.

Relevant schemes for general building work are those of the Building Employers Confederation and the Federation of Master Builders.

the BEC guarantee scheme
This scheme is operated by the BEC Building Trust, a subsidiary of the Building Employers Confederation (an organisation for contractors of a general building nature, both large and small). The guarantee scheme covers jobs between (at present) £500 and £35,000 involving all normal building and home improvement work including decorating, heating and electrical installations, kitchens and bathrooms. It provides the following:

○ full insurance of the work, goods and materials, for all damage from the day work starts
○ if the builder does not finish the work, another BEC member will be asked to complete the work
○ any faults that occur within 6 months after the work has finished will be put right by the builder (this is the defects liability period in the contract)
○ for a further 2 years, any 'structural' defect that occurs will be rectified; this would be a defect with the foundations or a load-bearing part of the roof, floor or wall
○ if the builder goes out of business, another BEC member will be called in to complete the work and/or put right defects during the liability period and if this costs more than what

you originally agreed to pay, the BEC scheme will pay up to a maximum of £5000 (plus VAT) for additional costs.

○ if you get into a dispute with the builder on any matter related to the contract, the BEC will appoint an independent professional qualified conciliator acceptable to both parties.

This guarantee scheme can be organised on your behalf by a builder who is a member of the BEC. The work must be carried out under a formal written contract: a special 'guarantee scheme' contract, approved by the Office of Fair Trading. The cost to you is a payment of 1% of the contract price (minimum fee £20).

If you request that the project is done under the scheme, so long as it qualifies, the builder must provide the facility — indeed, if you employ him directly he should suggest it to you. You must enter into the agreement before the work starts; you normally cannot enter the scheme once the job has begun.

Federation of Master Builders' Register
The FMB operates a warranty scheme called the 'National Register of Warranted Builders'. Being a member of the Federation does not mean that the builder is necessarily part of this scheme.

It covers any type of work up to a value of £50,000 including VAT, and must be entered into before the work has begun. The warranty provides the following:

○ for two years after the completion of the work, any defects through faulty workmanship or materials reported in writing to the Federation's registrar will, if agreed, be put right at no extra cost to you

○ if the builder becomes insolvent or the sole practitioner dies, the Federation will bring in another member to finish the work or rectify the defects; if the work costs more than you originally agreed, they will also pay up to £8,000 of additional costs

○ if a dispute occurs between you and the builder, the registration board provides a conciliation and arbitration service to reach a speedy and inexpensive decision. If you are found to be right and the builder does not carry out the works as instructed, the registration board will pay the reasonable costs of the work being done by another builder.

The cost of the scheme to you is 1% of the contract price, with a minimum fee of £5.

These schemes, in certain circumstances, can offer a measure of protection for your project but your aim should still be, from the very beginning and at all stages, to organise a project that will be as free as possible from problems. Don't sit back and relax just because you are using a builder who works under a warranty or guarantee scheme.

is one builder enough?

Whatever your scheme, whether it's a new building, an extension or a series of repair/improvement jobs, it will almost certainly consist of several different elements or trades. For instance, assume your building project will consist of the following:

1. replacement of several plaster ceilings
2. repair of external rendering
3. repair/replacement of the guttering and repair of the tiled roof
4. curing rising damp in the kitchen
5. fitting a new kitchen
6. putting in a downstairs w.c.
7. insulating the cavities of the external wall

8. rewiring the electrical system of the whole house
9. repairing and repainting the external wooden window frames.

Although this list is quite extensive and varied, it is typical of the sort of work people may wish to carry out on a neglected property.

You could end up employing six or more specialist individuals or firms to carry out these jobs:

○ a plastering firm or plasterer to do the ceilings/rendering
○ a roofer to do the gutters/roof
○ a specialist damp proofing firm for the rising damp
○ a kitchen-fitting firm
○ a plumber
○ insulation specialist for cavity walls
○ an electrician for the rewiring
○ a carpenter
○ a decorator

Obviously, if you were to employ separate firms to do each of these operations, the organisational problems would soon overwhelm you.

employing separate contractors

Many builders, even the small one-person firms, can do several of these jobs. In the example, one firm might be able to do the decorating, carpentry and plastering. But you would still be faced with the possibility of having to employ several different firms to carry out the full range of work. There are a few drawbacks with this:

○ *access for estimates* — if you want competitive quotes for all or several areas of the work, you will have to make arrangements with many different people, arranging to be in, giving information etc

○ *overlapping work* — in most building schemes, the different types of work will have an effect on the others. This could lead to split responsibilities. For example:

— The layout of the kitchen will determine where the electrical sockets will go. If the electrical work is not done when the kitchen fitters turn up, or the sockets have been put in the wrong place, the fitters will either fit the units regardless or go away without doing anything. This 'pulling off site' will mean extra charges for you.
— The kitchen problems don't stop there; the damp proofing firm will have to complete its work before the kitchen units are fitted.
— In the event of a mix-up, you'll probably find that each contractor blames the other for the delay, leaving you unable to work out who did what wrong. They will all probably end up making extra charges for wasted time.

This highlights only one area of possible confusion. The plumber, plasterer, decorator, insulation people and roofers could also become entwined.

limiting the contractors

One way of making life easier is to limit the number of separate firms that you employ. A scheme, such as the one described above can be separated into two different types of work:

○ building work that can be organised by a general builder
○ specialist work that builders are not usually equipped or trained to carry out.

building work
Taking the example described above, a general builder could organise and carry out the plastering, rendering, guttering and plumbing. Whether his own employees will actually do the

work depends on the size of the builder's firm and the range of skills of the staff. In most cases, the electrical work and possibly the roofing will be done by sub-contractors.

As long as they are sub-contractors whom the builder uses regularly, you should consider them as the builder's own staff. The builder will be responsible for co-ordinating their work, their standards and performance. If something goes wrong, it's up to the builder to put it right.

Another advantage with this method is that duplication of the work will be minimised. For instance, when the old plaster ceilings have been pulled down, the electrician will be able to put the wiring into the floor space from the underneath, saving time and money by not having to lift floorboards.

Contractors also prefer to work with other contractors they know. They have fewer worries about paying each other and about co-ordination.

specialist work

There are some parts of the work that the general builder would find unprofitable or would be unable to carry out. The equipment and training required would be too expensive when compared to the volume of jobs to be done.

Some contractors specialise in one particular area — replacement windows, fitted kitchens and bathrooms, for instance.

In the above example, specialists would normally be used to insulate the cavity walls, carry out the damp proofing and fit the new kitchen. Getting estimates from a couple of each of the specialists helps to give you an idea of the total cost, and is useful when you ask a builder to tender for the whole lot.

the 'grey' areas

Even using a general builder and specialists, you would still be employing four separate firms. You could consider rationalising this even further.

Many general builders are able to fit kitchen units, so you could consider buying the kitchen units direct and getting the builder to fit them. One drawback of this method is that the builder, although competent, may not be familiar with the particular type of kitchen units and how they should be put together. Also, the builder will need a plan to work from so you would need to choose a kitchen supplier who also offers a design service.

Although damp proofing is a specialised operation, many builders offer the service, carried out either by themselves or by a local sub-contractor.

You could consider 'nominating' the specialists to be sub-contractors to the main builder so that he co-ordinates them all.

the 'cost' of co-ordinating

If you ask a builder to co-ordinate the work of several other specialist contractors, you may find that he will make a charge for doing this. In some cases, the amount could surprise you, sometimes in the region of hundreds of pounds.

Many builders anticipate that this co-ordination will involve them in a lot of additional work such as writing letters, telephoning, arranging appointments, progress-chasing when operatives don't turn up. As much of this is office-based work, and time usually means money, they will include amounts of money within their quotation to cover themselves. Faced with additional charges of this type, you may wish to reconsider your approach, especially if your finances are tight. (But if you do the co-ordination yourself, you too will have to spend some money — for example, on telephone calls — and a lot of time, and use diplomacy.)

which way is best?

The best method of organising the work will largely depend on you.

○ If you have the time, energy and personality, employing several different firms could suit you better but will be harder work and potentially bring you into conflict with more people.
○ If you don't fancy this approach or haven't the time available, you should get a general builder to organise it all, but you must be prepared to pay the additional costs.

work done by specialist firms

Over the last few years, the home improvement market has been flooded by specialist firms offering a variety of services ranging from porches to kitchens, double glazing to stone cladding.

doorstep and telephone contractors

Many firms promote their products or services through door to door and/or telephone canvassing, inserts in papers and magazines or leaflets pushed through your door. Many are reputable but others are not so professional either in their selling techniques or the standard of the product. Many pay their sales team substantial commissions — a feature not likely to result in their giving 'best advice' to customers.

Just one sunday paper, for instance, included adverts for fitted bathrooms, fitted kitchens, home extensions, loft conversions, double glazing, central heating, conservatories, exterior textured wall finish.

Most of these companies offer a complete service, organising all the necessary trades and building operations. In some cases, where planning permission and building regulations approval are required, they undertake to get those for you. To many people, this is like a dream come true. Trying to co-ordinate a similar project yourself might appear too daunting: what better than a firm who does it all for you?

Before you post your 'tear off' strip to some anonymous post code, or say "yes" to the pleasant persuasive salesperson who has been drinking your coffee for the last three hours, consider carefully what they are offering.

Companies offering services of this type can be generally divided into two broad categories:

○ those offering a single product service e.g. double glazing, central heating
○ those offering a complete package service e.g. loft conversion, home extension, conservatories, fitted kitchens.

single product companies

A common single product company is the double glazing firm, operating in a very competitive market with what appears to be very attractive deals. Offers of free or low cost finance with big discounts if you sign up there and then are common.

If you are interested in double glazing, a new central heating system or stone cladding to the outside of your house, don't put all your eggs in one basket, shop around and get to know the market. If some salesperson tries to push you into signing an agreement before you've looked around, be firm, thank them for their information, ask them for their 'phone number and say that you will contact them should you want any more information. Above all, don't sign anything until you are sure it's the product you want at the price that's suitable.

The Office of Fair Trading booklet *Home Improvements* has a section about cancellation rights and warns that

> "Only in the following circumstances will you generally have a legal right to cancel a contract you have entered into.
> When you buy from a trader who has called at your home

without an appointment or who had made an unsolicited tele-phone call, you have 7 days in which you can cancel the contract and get back any money you have paid. This applies to goods you buy and to work you arrange to have done, provided it costs more than £35. It applies to home improvements such as kitchen units and double glazing, but not to new building work such as a home extension.

When you pay by credit, you have slightly different rights. Having signed a credit agreement at home after discussing the deal face to face with the trader, you have 5 days in which you can change your mind. You will receive by post a second copy of the contract or another notice of your cancellation rights: the 5-day 'cooling off' period runs from the day this arrives. So, make a note of the date.

You must be given written notice of any cancellation rights when you agree to buy, either by cash or credit. If you do want to cancel, act quickly. Write to the firm and, if possible, send the letter by recorded delivery."

Before you invite any firms around for a quotation, try to get some information on them. Your local authority trading stan-dards office or the citizens advice bureau might offer some comments. Ask the firms for references and check them out.

When investigating a product, service or contractor, obtain literature from the relevant trade association. This will provide information on product types available and give the genuine claims for the product or process under consideration. You can also ask for a list of contractors recognised by the association who operate to the association's code of practice and customer protection arrangements. If you are contacted direct by the contractor, or follow up an advertisement, it is wise to ring or write to the relevant association to check that the contractor or company is a current member.

Try to make sure that all the firms are quoting for similar work. For instance, asking three different firms to quote for timber, for PVC and for aluminium windows respectively won't be as useful as deciding on what type of windows you want first and then inviting three firms to quote for that type. Even with the same type, the quality of the product can vary tremendously. So,

○ try to see the product installed somewhere else, have a good look at it, open/close it, do you like the look and feel of it?
○ is the product covered by a British Standard? But be careful, they may stamp the BSI kitemark all over their adverts and literature but it may relate to only part of the product — the hinges or the glass, for instance. Ask precisely what the kitemark refers to.

And remember that a reputable builder can often obtain the same windows and fit them for you at a lower price and, if a warranted builder, with a longer guarantee.

Each firm will have its own type of agreement for you to sign, most probably a standard form. Read through the small print very carefully to see what contract conditions it contains. If you want any particular feature, or a firm date of completion, insist that it's written in or get a good reason why it cannot be.

Will any deposit that you are asked to pay be protected by, for example, an indemnity fund should the trader go out of business before the work is done?

Does the firm have any sort of warranty or guarantee for its products? If it does, how long is the guarantee period? What happens if the firm goes bankrupt — does the guarantee become worthless or is it protected by any back-up scheme?

What is the structure of the firm: where is it based? who is in charge? Some firms have very complex management structures: one person in charge of the selling, one in charge of the estimating, yet another in charge of the manufacture and another in charge of the installation process. Make sure you have all the relevant names and telephone numbers.

complete package companies

These firms carry out a variety of building operations. They should be selected and employed like any other builder. The main difference is that they usually offer a design service as well, and will obtain all necessary building regulations and planning approvals. You should check the following features of the firm:

○ If the firm operates on a national scale, ask about their organisation.

— Do they use their own employees to do all the work or do they employ local sub-contractors? If it's the latter, how do they control the work at such long distances?

— Do they take full responsibility for their workforce, be they full-time, sub-contracted or self-employed?

— Who will be responsible for the whole of your project? (with companies operating at full stretch geographically, supervision and control may be difficult)

— Are the people who design the project and prepare the application for planning permission and building regulations approval professionally qualified? do they have good local knowledge?

○ How are the design fees charged — a fixed price, separate from the construction costs or all lumped together?

○ What sort of contract is used? will you have a chance to look at it before you have to sign it?

Unless you get several similar firms to quote for similar designs, it will be difficult to compare the prices. The only relevant comparison would be with a similar scheme organised along traditional lines using a separate professional to design and organise the scheme and a builder to construct it.

getting a price for the work

To obtain the most competitive price for the work, you should ask more than one builder to quote for your scheme. You should ask for quotations rather than estimates, wherever possible. Quotes are preferable because they are immovable: whatever happens, that is the price that will subsequently be charged for the contracted work. Estimates, on the other hand, are not binding.

It costs money for the builder to price a job. He or some experienced member of the firm has to visit your property, measure up and work out the quote. You should ask only those builders you are genuinely interested in to quote and only when you are fairly sure that the job will go ahead. (If too many builders submit too many abortive quotes, the costs will be passed on to the consumer through higher building prices.)

You should ask all the builders to quote for more or less the same work. If you start changing your mind every time a different builder comes around, you will end up with prices that can't really be compared.

Warning: do not get one builder's detailed estimate, 'white out' the name and take it to other builders to get cheaper quotes. This is unethical and is one of the reasons why builders now often charge for estimates where no professional is involved.

the tendering procedure

The dictionary definition of a tender is an offer in writing to execute work or supply goods at a fixed price. Only ask for tenders from builders that you would like to do the job. As a rough guide, for work that you expect to cost up to £20,000, go to three builders; if likely to be over £20,000, you could increase this to four.

It's no good just sending the tendering documents to a builder without getting in touch with him first; he may be too busy or not interested in your type of work. Give the following information:

○ where the job is
○ what the likely value is
○ what the work involves
○ when you want the quotes back
○ when you would like the job starting and finishing.

Do all this well in advance of the time you want the builder to do the work: many builders are booked up for months in advance. The process from tendering through to starting the work can be many months. Also, everyone wants a builder to do work during the summer — a time, too, when builders take their holidays. So, get in there early: at least 3 to 4 months before you would like the work to start.

the documents

The tendering documents consist of the contract conditions, specification and any drawings that outline the scope of the work. You should ensure that each builder is sent exactly the same information.

You should include a covering letter suggesting arrangements for the builder to come and look at the house (to assess the site of the work and measure up etc). It would be useful for you to be there when each of them comes so that you can answer questions and consider alternatives. As you will be seeing more than one builder, make a note straightaway of what you discuss with each one.

Your letter should ask for how long the tender price is valid and whether the price is inclusive of VAT or will VAT be additional. You should state the date the quotes should be returned by.

The time allowed for tendering depends on the size and complexity of the job. For most small domestic jobs, 3 to 4 weeks should be long enough for most builders. You must not disclose one builder's quote to another builder before all tenders are submitted. In fact, you should open all the envelopes at the same time after the stated date to ensure fairness. It is unacceptable in the building industry to obtain a price from one builder and use that to try and get a lower price from another.

deciding which price to accept

When professionals ask for tenders, they hope that the tender documents are so clear that the builder has no problem in understanding them. The lowest price is therefore usually the one that they accept.

If you have prepared the documents yourself, you may not have been able to write a precise enough description of the work, and the builders might well quote on the basis of their own interpretation of what they think you want. For instance, against your description of the guttering repair required, the builder may have added in his own handwriting "clean out and re-make joints only". Or, where you've asked for re-point-ing the walls of your house, one builder may have added "Allow area of 50 sq. metres". Comments or qualifications of this nature might suggest that some of the work that's being priced for could be different to other quotes. If there does seem to be some difference between what they are quoting for, phone them to discuss and clarify what their price includes.

Once you appear to have a set of prices that will stand some comparison, you have to decide which builder to employ. It is common practice in the construction industry that, so long as the builder meets all your other requirements, the one who submits the lowest quote is awarded the contract. Ideally, you should follow this process as it could save you a great deal of money. You may find that the difference between the highest and lowest price is quite considerable.

When builders are very keen to do the work, they will cut their prices back to a minimum so that they stand a chance of winning. If they are busy and would rather not do the work, their quote will be high to try to ensure that they will not get the job.

If two builders have put in a price for installing a new door of £450 and of £520 respectively and the third has put down a price of £175, you should ask the lowest tenderer the reason for the big difference. Does his lower price indicate the use of inferior materials? a lack of knowledge of what is needed? or are the other two just expensive? If you feel clearly that the builder submitting the lowest price is not satisfactory and gives a bad impression in his approach to the work, consider employing the second lowest.

Should you choose a builder because he is a member of a trade organisation that operates a warranty/guarantee scheme or because he has good references or seems to you to have the right approach and competence? A warranty/guarantee scheme provides a good 'safety' net but by itself it does not ensure that the builder — and the project — will be a success.

appointing the contractor

Once you have decided on the builder whose price you are going to accept, you should arrange a meeting with the builder to discuss essential points: the most important aspects are when he can start, when he undertakes to finish, the stages in which he plans to do the work. If the scheme will entail long-term disruption, it may be possible to arrange for the work to be done in a sequence which will make the house at least habitable in parts throughout the duration of the works.

After this meeting, if all seems well, you should write a letter of appointment to the builder. In this, you should

○ confirm that you want to employ him to carry out the works as described in your contract documents (give reference numbers)
○ confirm the contract sum and that it is a fixed-price contract and that VAT is (or is not, as the case may be) extra
○ state the start and finish dates
○ confirm the payment arrangements
○ state any retention amounts.

The builder's tender was an 'offer' to carry out the work in accordance with the specification and the contract conditions and your letter will be the acceptance of that offer. This forms the contract between you.

getting ready for the work

Ideally, you should have already thought about the type of preparations you'll need to make for the work while you were planning the project. This will depend on your circumstances and the extent of the works. Typical preparations include:

○ sending the kids, elderly family members, those whose health might be affected, off to stay with friends/family for the course of the work
○ arrange for the pets to go to boarding kennels/neighbours/friends
○ pack away all breakable items, carpets etc and put them in

an area of the property that isn't going to be affected by the work
- buy/hire dust sheets to cover your furniture; move vulnerable furniture out of the way; if the works are extensive, put furniture into storage if necessary
- jewellery and other valuable items to be deposited with your bank in a safety deposit box or other place of safe keeping
- if you are storing any of your possessions in friends'/family homes, keep a note of where they are, tell your insurers and make sure that your insurance policy will continue to cover the items
- empty chests, shelves, cupboards that will have to be moved
- do not leave elaborate cooked meals or precious food in your deep freeze or fridge because a workman may switch off the mains and leave it off until the freezer contents have melted
- put your own tools away
- if the house is to be uninhabited while the workmen will be there and you are concerned about your telephone bills, you can ask the area telephone manager for outgoing calls to be barred until further notice (the charge for an 'o.c.b.' arrangement is £11)
- notify your neighbours of the likely start date; if the builder will need to work off their property, ask permission and give them the estimated date of this part of the work
- if the works are likely to affect deliveries (milk, papers, post) or refuse collection, make necessary arrangements with the people involved
- make sure your money is available to pay the builder.

Make clear arrangements with the builder about

- whether workmen can use your facilities e.g. kitchen, garage, sheds, lavatory
- where to store/put tools, equipment, delivered goods (NB ladders not be left around unsecured)

- where to park car(s), van, lorry
- if skip required, who is to hire this? (licence needed from local authority if to be parked on highway)
- electricity and water supply for the work (and for the household if supply needs to be cut off at any stage)
- whether your telephone can/cannot be used
- when work is to start (and end) each day
- when noisiest work should not be done
- being careful not to damage any precious plants or shrubs in the garden
- how the house keys are to be handed over/back each day if/when no one is in the house.

insurance

Inform your insurance company or insurance broker that work will be starting on such-and-such a date and make sure that the cover is extended according to your commitment under your contract with the builder. (If the work turns out to take longer than you expected, inform your insurers in writing as soon as you are aware of the extension and give them a revised completion date.)

Before the builder starts working on your property, ask to see a copy of his insurance policy. Ask him for evidence that it is current; do not rely on just a cover note. Ensure that it relates to the builder you have employed: it should have the builder's name mentioned somewhere in the schedule.

safety on site

All construction and demolition work is subject to the Health and Safety at Work etc Act 1974 and to certain provisions of the Factories Act 1961 and the various codes of regulations which apply to construction activities.

Under the provisions of the Health and Safety at Work etc Act, any builder who employs people has a responsibility to ensure so far as is reasonably practicable, the health and safety and welfare of all his employees, and a duty to carry out the work in a way that does not endanger other contractors' workmen or members of the public. Some builders take their legal responsibilities very seriously and make efforts to ensure that their operatives work in a safe manner. Other builders, however, may not be so careful and may attempt to carry out work in an unsafe manner, such as re-roofing a house using simple ladders rather than erecting a proper scaffold; failing to provide operatives with tools and equipment which are safe to use and with proper protective clothing such as safety helmets, goggles, hearing protectors, gloves, safety shoes; failing to take safeguards to prevent materials or tools falling on passers-by, neighbours, you and your family; failing to provide adequate welfare facilities such as washing facilities, site hut and first-aid box or alternatively failing to make suitable arrangements with the occupier of the premises to use existing facilities.

As the customer, provided you have included a requirement in your contract terms for the builder to ' . . . conform with all statutory requirements', it is up to the builder to make this provision. To cover yourself further, you should ask the builder whether his method of working will conform to health and safety legislation and is this included in the quote? If the answer is "yes", you should not entertain any claims for additional money should the builder be caught out by the Health and Safety Executive inspectors.

Inspectors have the power to stop the work by issuing a prohibition notice in cases where work is being carried out unsafely. This would inevitably lead to delays. Where the work is likely to last longer than six weeks, the builder has a legal duty to notify the local HSE inspector.

Further information may be obtained from a local office of the Health and Safety Executive (in the telephone directory) or from your local authority.

the work and your neighbours

Unless you live in an isolated farmhouse, your scheme will almost certainly affect your neighbours. A rear extension might cut out a bit of sunlight to their garden, a new window might overlook their property, the noise of the building work could get on their nerves. The impact will depend on

○ the type and extent of the work
○ the tolerance of your neighbour
○ your relationship with your neighbour.

If you show consideration and try to minimise the impact, relationships will be helped. If you don't get on with your neighbours, don't be tempted to ignore their interests. If planning permission is required, for instance, the council will inform them as a matter of course and invite comments. These comments, or objections, could delay the scheme if not stop it altogether.

Even if you don't need planning permission, some of the work may affect the structure between your properties or a common boundary line. Unhelpful neighbours could apply to the courts for an injunction to halt the work. If you already have a contract with a builder, the halting of the work could cost you a lot of money.

Once you have an idea of what you want to do, you should consider discussing the following issues with your neighbours:

○ *daylight* — any restriction in the amount of daylighting to your neighbour's home would have to cut out a great deal of light before the planning authority or the courts would act.

○ *access* — if your extension stops on or very near the boundary line, your builders will need access from your neighbour's side. They may need to erect scaffolding wholly on your neighbour's property. Unless you get his permission, your neighbour could deny access and effectively halt your work.

○ *dust, dirt etc.* — no matter how careful your builder, there is bound to be some debris and dust that will drift over to your neighbours' property. You could offer to clean your neighbours' windows, wash down their paths etc when the work is done. You should be especially careful of your neighbours' cars.

○ *noise* — building works are noisy no matter how considerate your builder is. Discuss with your neighbours whether they have any special requirements e.g. shift worker, infirm or sensitive occupants, what time they normally get up etc. Agree times when the noisiest work can be done. Ensure that your builder will use good, well-maintained, 'muffled' equipment to keep the noise to a minimum (and ask his men to keep their radios down). If your building work is unreasonably noisy, your neighbour could complain to the local authority's environmental health department who have powers under the Control of Pollution Act 1974 to instruct how the works should be carried out.

party walls

If you live in a semi-detached or terraced property, the wall between you and your neighbour is the 'party wall'. Basically, imagine a line drawn down the centre of the 'party wall': that is where the 'boundary' of ownership starts and stops. The ownership of this wall is complex and you and your neighbour's rights in relationship to it vary depending on where in the country you live.

This party wall not only relates to the wall but also extends down to the foundations and up through the roof covering as well. If the roof tiles are continuous from one property to another and straddle the party wall, these features should be included under the party wall discussions.

Broadly speaking, you can carry out whatever work you want to without telling your neighbour so long as you don't interfere with his 'rights'. These rights include the right of support. You can't dig away the foundations of the party wall allowing it to collapse, for instance. Neither can you impose additional 'weight' or 'load' on to the wall that would make the foundations give way. These examples are extreme. Many other types of work may affect your neighbour's side of the wall and so should be discussed and agreed if possible:

○ taking out a chimney breast on your side of the wall: because your neighbours will almost certainly have one on their side, you must ensure that you don't affect the structural stability

○ re-covering your roof if the tiles are interlinked with your neighbour's: you must make sure not to damage the tiles on his side of this junction

○ hacking off old plaster, knocking new openings in walls of your property near to the party wall, breaking up of old solid floors and other semi-demolition work carried out by mechanical equipment must not cause cracking in the wall or plaster surfaces on your neighbour's side

○ the injection of a chemical damp proof course could affect your neighbour's side because of the heavy drilling and injection of fluid.

You should discuss the proposed work with your neighbours, however minimally you think it might affect them.

The more 'structural' the work you propose, the more chance of damage to your neighbour's property unless your builders are very careful. A reliable and experienced builder can offer advice but you may have to consider getting professional advice (from, for example, a building surveyor).

inspecting the party wall

If you or your neighbour think that the work could have an effect on the party wall, you should take the precaution of inspecting your neighbour's side of the wall. This will help prevent disputes in the future should any damage occur. Imagine the situation if you don't check, your builder carries out the work and the neighbour slaps a court order on you claiming that vibrations affected his roof covering, causing leaks that resulted in hundreds of pounds-worth of damage. How will you defend yourself? If you have an accurate record of the condition prior to the work being carried out, you could be more prepared.

When you inspect the property with your neighbour, both of you should agree, as far as possible, the present condition of the building. You should inspect their side of the party wall, the ceilings and other walls adjacent to it. The sort of things you should note include

○ the type and standard of decorations: whether they are in good condition, fair or in need of redecoration
○ the position of any existing cracks in walls and/or ceilings and, if possible, their length
○ any damp stains on the ceilings or walls, their location and approximate size
○ any unusual features or fittings e.g. large fixed mirrors, panelling, pictures etc.
○ fireplaces
○ pipework.

You should write these down, room by room, and both you and your neighbour should sign and date the document at the end and each keep a copy.

If your builder will be hammering or drilling on the party wall, you should advise your neighbour to take certain precautions to help prevent any damage. These might include

○ taking down any pictures, mirrors, wall lights etc
○ clearing any shelves on the party wall of delicate or valuable objects.

You could offer to help with these preparations.

If the neighbours have any open fires, get your builder to cover up the front with plastic sheeting or paper taped on so that soot or dust won't fall into the room, and to clean up afterwards.

after the work

When the work has finished, you should arrange another joint inspection with your neighbours to see if there has been any damage to their side of the wall. Using the original inspection notes and any photos, you should look to see if any cracks have developed or extended, roof leaks started etc.

If nothing appears to be amiss, get your neighbour to confirm by signing the inspection note. This is the easy bit — but if there has been any damage, what should happen then? This will depend on the extent of the damage and the attitude of your neighbour.

You should try to determine whether the damage is due to the work carried out on your side. If a roof leak developed or got worse in a bedroom on the second floor but your work involved hacking off a bit of plaster on the ground floor, it's unlikely that the two are connected. But if you were having a new staircase put in and all the plaster had fallen off the other side of the party wall in a corresponding position, the two events could be connected.

If both of you agree that damage has occurred through reason of the works, you should seek to agree what should be done about it.

If a ceiling has fallen down or wall plaster fallen off, you might offer to pay a builder to put it right. If a crack in a wall or ceiling has got worse i.e. a little bit wider and longer, and it is bad enough for your neighbour to claim for redecoration, you have to decide how much redecoration — the ceiling only or the walls as well. If the ceiling was already wet and stained before the work, you have to decide whether to offer any compensation if it's got only a little bit worse.

The accent will be on negotiation. If there has been a little damage but the decorations were quite grotty anyway, you could offer to buy a couple of tins of paint when they next redecorate. If they redecorated only last year and a big crack now appears down the wall, you could agree to pay for the crack to be made good and to redecorate that wall.

Before you begin to offer any money or to arrange such repair work, check to see whether your or your builder's insurance policy covers the damage under the liability sections.

There is a RICS Guidance Note *Party wall legislation and procedure* (£4.95 from RICS bookshop), dealing specifically with prescribed procedures for inner London but recommending that for properties outside the London Building Acts' area, it could be "beneficial to all parties" to follow similar procedures.

party walls in London and other local variations

For most areas of the country, the law relating to party walls is mainly contained in the Law of Property Act 1925 and is not very specific. In some cities, local statutes exist that specifically control the works to a party wall. You could ask your local authority's building control department or legal department whether there are any local statutes or byelaws of this nature in your area.

Take London, for instance. Because buildings have been so densely packed together for so long, legislation concerning the rights of adjoining owners have existed since medieval times. The current party wall regulations are contained in the London Building Acts (Amendment) Act (1939). These impose specific rights and duties on the owner carrying out the works ('the building owner') and his neighbour ('the adjoining owner') and specify the process involved.

You must make sure that all adjoining owners are notified before you start work. This is important when you live in a block of flats where you are surrounded by adjoining owners. If notification is not given, the neighbours could stop you carrying out the work.

The Act provides for the liability for payment for works to party structures, which means that your neighbour may have to pay for some of your building work, where there is joint benefit.

The building owner must send details of the proposals to the adjoining owner a minimum of two months before the work starts. Discussions and negotiations concerning these proposals are carried out and, when agreement is reached, a 'party wall award' is drawn up that outlines the scope of the work precisely. Before the work goes ahead, a joint inspection is carried out to agree the condition of the party wall. The work can then go ahead, supervised by the building owner but with the adjoining owner having the right to inspect as well. After the work has been completed, the party wall is inspected to see if any damage has occurred. If it has, compensation is negotiated.

In cases of dispute, the Act lays down that surveyors shall be appointed to ensure compliance with the Act. The surveyors' fees are payable by the owner carrying out the work.

In Scotland, there are similar procedures but adapted to suit flatted and tenement blocks, a common type of property there.

while the work is being done

Since you will not have a professional administering the contract for you, to some extent you'll have to take that role. But do not try to be an architect or surveyor: if you do, it will soon become obvious that your technical and contractual knowledge isn't up to it and you'll quickly lose control and respect.

Your role should be that of an informed client, aware of the contract conditions and what you want out of the scheme but prepared to leave the technical aspects to the builder.

on site

Unless you see something that is obviously in breach of your agreement with the builder (e.g. they start painting the house purple instead of white or they are playing a radio very loudly at 6.45am when you stipulated that they shouldn't), you should not get too involved with the day to day progress of the work. Suggest to the builder that you have formal meetings, perhaps once a week, when you can discuss any matters that concern you.

If workmen are to be on your premises for a period of time, try to ensure common courtesies are upheld throughout the period.

The chap who is in charge of the actual work may not be the one with whom you have been negotiating. Make sure you know who is responsible for daily activities, and establish a working relationship with him. Refer any queries or complaints to him rather than to any of the other workmen who come and go. And get him to contact you should any unexpected problems arise needing an instant decision (make sure he has your telephone number at work).

React quickly to the builder's requests or comments, but don't be rushed. Although you should not hold up the work, nothing is likely to be so urgent that it cannot wait until tomorrow. This will give you time to think the matter over and come to a reasoned decision.

Try to keep a daily log of how the work is progressing and what the workmen have done — or not done.

The sort of things that you can watch for include

○ if any special materials or fittings are stored on site waiting to be fixed into position, are they properly protected from damage? For instance, is your new hardwood-topped kitchen unit being used as a breakfast bar or are your new veneer-faced doors left out in the rain?
○ that the workmen are conforming to any special conditions you might have included in the terms of the contract.

If they have done something that you are not sure about, make a note of it and discuss it with the builder at your regular meeting. Even if you are sure that something is wrong, be tactful with your questions — builders can be very sensitive to criticism.

When you walk around to inspect the works, be very careful. Building sites can be dangerous places, even for just a small project. Exposed electric cables, excavations, unprotected scaffolding, unsecured ladders can cause injury to anyone not aware of these dangers. Ideally, you should get the builder's permission to look around the site.

extra work and rises in costs

You should stipulate that the builder informs you of all extra work he considers necessary before it is carried out. If you make this demand, you should ensure that the builder can contact you relatively quickly i.e. the same day. If the extra work is preventing them getting on with the rest of the work, a delay in contacting you will delay the job as a whole.

When the need for extra work occurs, ask the builder

○ what is the nature of the work?
○ why wasn't it included in the original quote?
○ does this work have to be done — what are the consequences if it isn't?
○ are there any different ways of solving the problem?
○ how much will the extra work cost?

The answers to some of these questions may sound very technical to you. If you are confused, ask the builder to explain them to you in terms you understand.

If the costs are rising so much that your financial limit is approaching, discuss with the builder methods of reducing the costs of the rest of the scheme by either cutting out work or substituting less expensive materials.

After a discussion on the telephone or face to face, ask the builder to confirm the extent and cost of the extra work in writing as soon as possible. As a back-up, you should keep a 'duplicate book' at hand, so that you can note any further instructions that you have agreed with the builder. Make sure you date the instruction. Give the top copy to the builder and retain the book. If you follow this method on every occasion, it is fair to say to the builder that you won't pay for any extra work unless it has been agreed. What you need to avoid is the builder at the end of the job giving you a long list of extra works that you knew nothing about.

inspections by the building control officer

While the work is going on, the building control officer from the local authority will inspect the work at various stages to make sure that the work is meeting the requirements of the Building Regulations.

Strictly, it is your duty to inform the building control officer whenever any change in method or materials has been made so that he can check whether this alteration complies with the Building Regulations. He should notice any differences during his stage inspections, but by that time it may be costly to correct any non-compliance with the regulations.

The building control officer can ask for additional work to be done because of the requirements of the Building Regulations. These requirements can lead to extra costs. For instance, your builder had dug a foundation trench to a depth of one metre as previously agreed. The building control officer inspects the trench and considers that the soil is not able to support the weight of the building and tells the builder to dig down another 0.5 metre until firmer ground is reached. In such a case, there is little choice; you will have to conform to the building control officer's requirements.

Building control officers are helpful people who are generally keen to suggest better and possibly cheaper ways of getting around problems. At the start of the work, you should find out which building officer will be inspecting the work on your property and establish contact.

variations and additions

Apart from extra work arising from necessity, you may get an idea or see an opportunity for something extra. In this case, you should discuss it with the builder and ask for a quotation for this item of work as soon as possible. Do not rely on an 'off the cuff' verbal estimate while discussing the matter on site.

pricing extra work

Pricing of additional work is the cause of many building contract disputes. There is always the worry that, because the builder is not quoting in competition, the cost of the extra work will be over the top. There is no easy way to check these prices unless you are familiar with current building costs. A few simple rules may help.

Does the original quote include items of work that are similar in nature to the extra work? For instance, if the ceiling in the lounge has to be replaced unexpectedly and the builder has already quoted for replacing the kitchen ceiling, the 'rate' for this work can be applied to the additional item. The calculation below illustrates this:

kitchen ceiling: size 4 metres × 3 metres = 12 sq. metres
cost of item in original quote = £120
therefore, cost per square metre = £10 per sq. metre

lounge ceiling: size 7 metres × 4 metres = 28 sq. metres
cost per sq. metre at kitchen rate = £10 per sq. metre
therefore, cost of lounge ceiling should be 28 × 10 = £280.

This method provides a basic check to test whether the price of the extra work is reasonable or not. But where the two items of work are not exactly the same, the builder could claim that more preparation etc work has to be done. Sometimes extras will involve out-of-sequence working which will increase the costs above the rate quoted. For example: new copper pipework, in sequence = quarter of an hour's work; renew 1 metre of pipework elsewhere out of sequence, involving special separate visit by plumber = 1 day's work.

The cost of building work consists mainly of two elements, the cost of the materials and the cost of the labour required to do the work.

Ask the builder to provide a breakdown of the cost of any

additional work into these two parts. You can check the cost of the materials by looking through a price list from a DIY store or builders merchants. But you have to allow for the builder to add profit and overheads to this materials cost.

The labour content is a bit more difficult. This element is basically the amount of time (in hours) that the operatives actually take to do the work, multiplied by the 'cost' of those operatives per hour. This 'cost' is not just the wages that they get in their pay packets, but includes the builder's overheads i.e. office expenses, national insurance contributions, transport, profit element etc. So, although the carpenter may get paid £3.50 per hour, you might be charged £8 per hour for his time.

Assessing the time any item of extra work takes is difficult unless you are familiar with that operation. You should apply common sense. If your builder is charging for ten hours to repair a leaking tap, you could be forgiven for questioning the amount. If the builder points out that the tap is an old pattern, he had to chase around town trying to get a replacement, then had to strip the fitting down, grind the seating and repair four other leaking joints beneath the sink, maybe this doesn't seem too unreasonable.

It is always useful to agree a rate for labour cost and the percentage that is going to be added to the materials costs, before the work starts.

paying the builder

You should agree terms of payment beforehand with the builder, and make sure that you will have the necessary money available as soon as payment is needed.

The method of payment will vary from builder to builder

and job to job. If the scheme is small and is likely to be completed within 3 to 4 weeks, the builder may be happy to be paid in full at the end of the job. If the contract will last longer, the builder might request staged or interim payments.

Whatever the arrangement, you should not pay a builder before work is started. A properly organised and financed builder will be able to progress the work for several weeks without having to ask for payments. If a builder asks you for money up front " . . to go and get some materials", his financial status may be suspect: it could be a sign that bankruptcy is on the way.

The exception to this rule would be where you employ a 'specialist' or a firm that carries out a particular type of work — for instance, double glazing, fitted kitchen, cavity wall insulation. It has become traditional that firms operating in these areas usually request a deposit before work is started. Or the builder may have to pay in advance, for example, for kitchen units. If so, you could give him a cheque payable to the kitchen unit company.

interim payments

If you agree to pay the builder in stages, you should only pay the value of the work that has already been done and of any materials that are on site. If you pay for something that has not been done and the builder disappears off the face of the earth, you'll have to pay again to get that part of the work finished. The builder may ask to be reimbursed for payment that he has made to special suppliers or to other sub-contractors: for example, a damp proofing firm.

Checking the value of the amount of work completed could be difficult for you but an informed guess can be made. Look at the builder's original quote and assess how much of it has been completed. Some parts of the work will be more costly than others, so you should discuss the proportion with the builder.

Although you should take care not to over-pay, you should also take care not to under-pay. If you refuse to pay a 'reasonable' amount, the builder could have cause to end the contract and sue you for any financial loss he has suffered. Again it's a question of reasonableness; you should endeavour to protect your own interests while honouring your obligations.

If your original contract documents stated that a percentage retention will be withheld, this should be deducted from the interim payment.

value added tax

All the costs of the work will be subject to value added tax at the standard rate (15% now) if the builder is VAT-registered. The builder will normally bill you for the cost of the work and VAT together, but he may submit separate invoices, one for the works and another for the VAT. You should always check the arithmetic just in case the calculations are incorrect.

Be careful if the builder has purchased any special fittings on your behalf such as kitchen units or bathroom suite and has included these 'p.c. sums' as part of a general payment, charging you VAT on them. Ask for a copy of the invoice for those items and make sure that they are adjusted net of VAT. The builder would have paid VAT on that cost and will charge you VAT on the total cost of the work.

when the work is done

The builder should tell you when he considers the job is complete. Go carefully around the new work on your own before organising a meeting between the two of you to discuss any snags. Without technical knowledge, it's difficult to be sure that you are picking up anything that is wrong. While you are occupying yourself with a few grubby marks on some wallpaper, the builder could be sweating over a wall that he knows isn't straight.

A few tips may help:

○ first of all, inspect the work with your original specification in hand and tick off the various headings of work that have been completed. Then carry out detailed inspection of each aspect to make sure that all the contract work has actually been finished.

○ floor, wall and ceiling finishes should be inspected for dirty marks, blemishes and unevenness. Look at these surfaces from different angles — sometimes the difference in the way the light hits a surface shows up defects

○ check all panes of glass to make sure none is cracked, especially in the corners

○ open and close all kitchen units, external and internal doors, windows, locks and bolts to make sure they operate without sticking

○ make sure doors have been fitted with enough gap underneath to ensure that they will clear any carpets

○ with new plumbing installations, fill the bath, sink and basins with water until it begins to spill into the overflow. Leave the water running for a while to see if the overflow pipe leaks. Pull the plug out and, where you can, look at the pipes underneath to see if any water is leaking there. Flush the w.c. to see if it works properly and look for any leaks.

○ test all electric sockets with an ordinary table lamp; switch on and off all light switches, extractor fans and any other special fittings. But do not rely on the light or power working as a proof of safety: test the operation of any miniature circuit breakers and residual current devices by activating and then resetting the device.

○ turn on the central heating and make sure that all the radiators warm up and the water gets hot and thermostats and water temperature controls are working; listen for knocks and other noises

○ beneath any roof that has been re-covered, look out for any new stains on the ceiling or at the top of the walls. When it's raining, go out and look at the gutters to see if any are leaking or blocked up. If you can easily look over a flat roof, make sure that there are no large puddles standing around for a long time; this can be bad for the roof covering.

Apart from these hints, use your common sense. Don't aim to set too high or too low a standard for the finished work but settle for a 'reasonable' standard, bearing in mind your original brief and the overall standard required. If you asked for a first class job, then you should expect that. But if you asked for an economical job, you should not expect first class.

If you do discover any defects, note down

○ the description of the defect
○ its location.

Make a list in your duplicate book, give a copy of the list to the builder and keep the original. You should agree a reasonable time limit for these defects to be put right, and inspect again when the builder notifies you that the work has been done.

In formal contract terms, the proper name for when the builder has finished the work is 'practical completion'. The term 'practically complete' means that the work is complete enough for the purposes it is meant for.

For example, assume that you've employed a builder to construct a new kitchen extension. You inspect the extension and you find that all the work is done apart from a kitchen unit door that is missing (due in two weeks) and a few areas of the new wall that you ask the builder to redecorate properly.

These defects are minor in nature and your kitchen is quite usable although the contract is technically not finished. It would be unreasonable to hold back the final instalment for these items. It would be better to knock off a sum of money that would cover the decorations and the kitchen unit door should the builder not return, and release the rest apart from the agreed retention.

Be reasonable: one mistake many people make when they are disputing the cost of some aspect of the work or the standard of finish, is that they hold back all or most of the outstanding money. If you are not happy with part of the work, hold back the value of only that item if possible.

If the contract conditions stated that a smaller amount of retention will be held during the defects liability period (for example, reducing from 5% down to $2\frac{1}{2}$%), you should release all other money due to the builder. For instance, if you are holding $2\frac{1}{2}$% retention, your payments to the builder (adding together the present and previous payments) should come to $97\frac{1}{2}$% of the total contract sum plus any extra work costs you may have agreed.

The resulting figure should represent the outstanding amount now payable to the builder. Assuming that any price changes are what you agreed, you should pay the account, promptly. If a retention is kept back, this should be paid at the end of the defects liability period, when any defects have been put right.

defects liability period

Without a professional's advice, you will have to exercise your own judgement over several issues during the defects period. Although the procedure is the same as described in pages 76 to 78, there will be a number of additional factors.

Firstly, you should ensure that you give the proper notifications to the builder. Once the 'snags' have been completed and you are happy about the job, that is the date the defects period runs from. You should write to the builder stating the start and end dates of the defects period which should be the same as stated in your contract conditions.

The builder is responsible for repairing or putting right any defect that occurs with the work during the defects period. The key phrase here is '. . . with the work'. This is not always as clear as the statement. For instance, if the contract involved the building of a kitchen extension, any problems with this distinct structure will have to be put right by the builder. But if the contract involved mainly repair work, it may not be so easy. If when the roof was overhauled, a number of tiles were replaced and one falls off after only two months, was it one that the builder replaced or one of the original ones that wasn't touched? If you call out the builder for a defect that wasn't part of the original contract, you may be faced with an extra charge.

response time
When you notice a defect, telephone the builder and inform him of the precise nature of the defect and discuss, and agree if possible, the course of action the builder intends to take, and when. Confirm all these details in writing to the builder as soon as possible, by first class post.

Response times are important in relation to defects. It is common knowledge that it is difficult to get builders back to put right defects on a job they have finished. By that time they are probably working on another job and are reluctant to spend time on jobs that don't have a direct income. If the defect is non-urgent, such as a crack in new plaster finish or some paint flaking off external window frames, it may be reasonable to wait until the end of the defects period to get the work done. If the defect is more urgent, such as a leaking pipe or roof, a door lock that doesn't work or heating in winter that has broken down, you should expect a quicker service. On these occasions, a response time of two working days is not unreasonable, less if the situation is very urgent.

You could agree with the original builder, if he cannot come to you easily, that you get a local man to do the repair and take the payment out of the retention money due to the builder.

If the original builder does not respond satisfactorily, and the defect requires urgent attention, you could consider employing another builder to do the work. Make sure you telephone the original builder first and inform him that you intend to instruct another builder and to charge the bill to him. Confirm this in writing as soon as possible.

at the end

Approximately two weeks before the end of the defects period, you should write to the builder arranging an inspection of the work. At this joint inspection, you should have a list of all the defects you have noticed since the contract was 'completed' and give a copy of this to the builder. If the defects are minor, the builder should be able to finish the items within two weeks.

If there were no defects, or when the builder has put right the listed defects to your satisfaction, the outstanding retention money should be paid to him within 14 days.

final account

The final cost of any contract will almost certainly be different from the original contract sum. At the end of the contract, the builder should give you a statement of the contract cost — the 'final account'. This should show

○ the original contract sum
○ the cost of any additions or omissions

○ any retention held back during the defects liability period
○ the final adjusted contract sum.

From this total should be deducted any interim payments made.

If the contract included for damages to be deducted if the work was not finished by a certain date, and it was not, the specified amounts can be deducted from any outstanding payments due.

not finishing on time

At all your meetings with the builder, you should have been asking whether there will be any problem about finishing within the contract period. This means that if the scheme does over-run, you will have had advance notice.

If the contract period is approaching its end and the work looks far from finished, you should check the following:

○ was the completion date clearly stated in the original documents?
○ did you ask the builder to do any extra work over and above that described in the original documents? or did the need for extra work become apparent during the course of the contract?
○ if there was extra work, was it just a few small items that could be done in sequence with the main work?
○ was the weather especially bad at the time when external works were being done?
○ did the builder inform you in writing or even verbally that the work might be delayed?
○ was the work progressed 'normally' or did the workmen not attend for long periods of time?

The object of asking these questions is to try and assess whether the delay is reasonable and beyond the builder's control. You should ask the builder to let you know the reasons for any delay as soon as possible and to provide a revised completion date.

Contractors do have genuine problems that even the most efficient cannot control, such as

— illness or death of a key workman
— absenteeism
— materials not delivered as promised
— materials delivered different to those ordered.

You must exercise some discretion and reasonableness, but try to check on excuses proffered.

If you are not happy with the explanation, write to the builder stating that you intend to deduct 'damages' from all outstanding payments as from

○ the contractual completion date, or
○ that date plus any agreed additions of time

until the work is agreed as being actually finshed. Remember, you can deduct damages only if they were stated in your original documents AND they represent actual loss to you.

later defects

Once you have finished with the builder, you should still keep an eye on the work the builder has done. Defects can occur a long time after the contract has been completed and, in some cases, the original builder may be liable for these latent defects.

The normal time limit imposed by the law for making a claim is 6 years from the time a negligent action occurred. But because of the nature of building work, where faults may not come to light for some time, under the Latent Damage Act 1986, you can make a claim for up to 3 years from the time the damage was discovered, even if that is longer than the normal

6-year limitation period. This issue is technically and legally complicated and you should go to a solicitor and a surveyor for advice on how to proceed.

Examples of latent defects would be

○ cracks that occur in brick walls because the foundations were not constructed properly
○ roofs that begin to sag because the builder didn't strengthen the structure as he should have done
○ complete heating systems that break down because the wrong components were used.

Don't confuse a latent defect with general deterioration in the building over time. What count as latent defects are generally serious structural faults or other defective work by the builder which was not apparent at the time. If all the paint begins to flake off your windows after a year or two, or your flat roof begins to leak slightly after five years, it is probably not worth taking any action despite your irritation at the work not standing the test of time.

For some items, there may be a long-term guarantee or extended warranty that you may be able to invoke: for example, for some heating installations, damp proof treatment, timber infestation treatments.

when things go wrong

If the builder is not proceeding with the work satisfactorily, give fair warning that you are considering cancelling the contract with him and employing another builder.

discharging the builder

You may have to get another builder in to finish off or put right the original builder's work because the original builder

○ fails to progress the work properly
○ fails to complete the work within the time
○ 'pulls off site' — simply stops turning up
○ does not put right work not properly done at the end of the contract
○ does not return to put right any defects that have occurred within the defects liability period
○ has gone bankrupt or died.

Even if you feel that the builder isn't likely to respond to your requests, you should go through certain procedures just in case the matter gets to court. You should aim to create the image of a reasonable but assertive person — even if you are not.

Meet or telephone the builder if possible, tell him what you think is wrong and ask him what action he will take, and when. Make a note of the date and time of the contact or the number of unsuccessful attempts.

If the builder doesn't do the work properly or doesn't turn up at all, write a letter outlining the sequence of events and clearly stating what actions you require the builder to take. State that if these actions aren't carried out within 14 working days, you will employ another builder to carry out the works and charge the cost against any outstanding payments due to the original builder. Send this letter by recorded delivery.

If you don't get any response within the 14 days, write another letter referring to the last letter and stating that since he is now in breach of contract, you intend to get another builder in to finish the work. You will have to pay him for no more than the work done so far, not the full contract sum.

Tell the builder to make arrangements for picking up any equipment on site. (Make sure you store any such equipment safely. Any materials on your property are probably yours as long as they relate to the work you're having done.) Send this final letter, too, by recorded delivery.

If you find out the builder has gone bankrupt, or has died and was the sole owner, things will get a bit complicated. In such a case, you should seek legal advice as soon as possible to make sure your rights are fully protected.

getting another builder in

If the original builder doesn't respond to your letters and you employ another to finish off the work, you should proceed with care to ensure that you do not prejudice your rights. In many cases, where the money value of the contract is small, the original builder just won't be bothered. If the amount of money at stake is more sizeable, you could find the builder resisting your moves and possibly embarking on legal action against you for breaking the contract yourself. If you have acted properly, don't let this response put you off but go to your own solicitor for advice.

When you employ another builder, make sure that

○ the second builder carries out only those works described in the original documents that haven't been done by the first builder

○ when asking the other builder to quote, he is aware that it is completion work resulting from a former contract
○ the costs of the second builder are 'reasonable', based on quotes from at least two builders.

You should attempt to draw up a statement of account for the work carried out by the original builder. Check how much of the work has been completed and, using the original specification, try to work out a total cost. You should add in the value of any materials that are on site and any payments that the original builder made on your behalf — for example, to gas board, suppliers, specialist treatment firm. A lot of this may be 'guesstimating' when, for instance, a floor is only half-built or a wall half-plastered.

If you have already given the first builder an interim payment for the work that has been done, less retention, do not make any more payments until you have adjusted the account. If you haven't paid the builder anything yet but an amount of work has been done, you should assess a fair amount, and pay that.

Once the work has been finally completed by the second builder, you should calculate whether it cost more than if it had been done by the original builder. Take the original contract sum, and deduct the value of the work carried out by the first builder. If the result is less than the amount that you've had to pay the second builder, you should seek to recover the difference from the original builder.

EXAMPLE

Original contract sum	£8,538
Value of work carried out by first builder	£2,345
	£6,193
Cost of employing second builder	£7,293
Loss to be recovered from original builder	£1,100

This could involve taking legal action, so you should consult your solicitor. You will have to be able to prove that costs are genuine and that like compares with like. You cannot sue a one-man firm for the extra amount it cost you to employ a substantial firm to complete the job.

help and advice

You can get some independent advice, should you need it, at the local citizens advice bureau. The local authority trading standards office may be able to help and will, in any event, be interested to learn of cases of misdescription of goods, and in some cases, of services provided. There may be infringements of criminal legislation such as the Trade Descriptions Act, which should be brought to the attention of the appropriate authority.

You could ask a local professional (architect, surveyor, consultant) if he would give advice in the dispute. Check the cost, however: the professional is unlikely to be willing to negotiate a competitive fee for his work in putting right what he considers is a shambles.

You should be familiar with your original agreement or contract and the work you asked to be done. And you should have made a note of extra work, variations, quotes, delays etc and the dates that they occurred.

from a guarantee scheme
If the original builder is a member of the Building Employers Confederation or of the Federation of Master Builders and was doing the work under their guarantee or warranty scheme and it comes to engaging another builder to finish the work for you, check the scheme's requirements about using another member for the work so that you can benefit from the payment by the scheme towards any costs in excess of the original contract price.

You may wish to invoke the scheme's conciliation service, and/or use the arbitration procedure, in order to reach settlement of a dispute between you and the builder.

Under the BEC Building Trust scheme, for instance, the appointed conciliator will visit the site and question both you and the builder on the nature of the disagreement, asking you what kind of solution you would agree to. The conciliator will then submit a report with recommendations on how the problem can be solved (copy of which you will receive). Apart from a refundable deposit of £25 from you, the scheme pays the cost of this conciliation.

If either you or the builder do not agree with the conciliator's recommendations or if the recommendations are accepted but not carried out, either party may ask for arbitration under the scheme's arbitration rules. These are a shortened form of documents-only arbitration, involving a written claim, defence, and claimant's reply. The arbitrator may or may not, at his discretion, visit the site. Arbitration has legal standing and results in a binding award. Neither party may ask for arbitration unless the matter has first been referred to conciliation; the parties may, however, do so by mutual consent.

If an arbitrator is appointed, a £50 deposit will be payable; if the arbitrator finds in your favour, this will be returned.

when it is your fault

The builder can 'determine' (end) the contract if

○ you, or anyone you are responsible for, interferes with or obstructs the work
○ you fail to make the premises available for the contractor when agreed
○ you stop the work for a continuous period of one month or more

○ you fail to make any payment within the time set in the contract (say, 14 days of the payment being properly due)
○ you become bankrupt.

If any of these happen, the builder will be able to make claims against you for any losses that he may have incurred. This could prove expensive, so be aware of your obligations under the contract and make certain that you can honour them.

Emergency repair work

When you have got plenty of time to plan your building work, you stand a good chance of success. You can work out what you want, what sort of builder to employ and how much it is likely to cost. But this will not always be the case. You might wake up one night to find water pouring through the ceiling from a plumbing or roof leak. You might return home after a day out to discover your windows have been smashed by vandals or your door locks forced by burglars. High winds can cause a variety of emergencies ranging from stripping of tiles off roofs to houses being demolished by falling trees.

In these circumstances, you have very little choice and not much time. All you'll want is a builder round quickly to get you out of the mess you're in. Because these disasters always seem to occur during the night and/or over weekends or bank holidays, the repairs can be very costly.

avoiding emergencies

Many emergency repair problems are caused by lack of proper preventive maintenance of the property. For instance,

○ old faulty wiring that you never got checked leading to blowing of the main fuse or, in the worst cases, a fire

○ badly insulated water pipework in unheated areas of the house freezing and bursting during cold weather

○ a few tiles on a roof having slipped or missing, high winds getting under the adjacent tiles and ripping them off, turning a slow leak into a deluge.

Many of these can be avoided if you regularly check over your property and carry out any necessary repairs.

If the owner fails to take reasonable steps for preserving a listed building, the local authority may be entitled to buy it compulsorily, or repair it and recover the cost from the owner. The Society for the Protection of Ancient Buildings can be asked for advice on what to do or not to do to a listed building.

If you have just moved into a new place or you feel you've neglected the one you are in, here's a check list that may help you.

water

Get to know the plumbing system in your house; use a DIY book to find out what tank is where and which pipe does what, and where all the stopcocks/valves are. (A good idea is to label pipes and stopcocks.) Check that they work properly. There is nothing worse than discovering that you can't turn a stopcock off when the water's pouring on your head or lapping round your feet. Turn each one on and off a few times and make sure that they don't leak themselves; sometimes a stopcock that hasn't been operated for a long time can cause a problem. If any of them don't work or are very difficult to operate, call in a plumber to replace/repair them.

If you haven't got enough stopcocks on your plumbing system to isolate the water properly and to shut the water off quickly in case of a leak, get some additional ones installed. As a minimum you should have

○ one on the cold water main either just outside or just inside your property
○ one on the cold water main just before it enters any cold water storage tank
○ one on the cold water supply pipe that comes off the cold water storage tank.

Make sure that all water pipes are well insulated where they are in unheated areas of the property. Don't skimp, get good quality insulation properly fixed. Don't take any chances: even the smallest bit of exposed pipe can let the frost in. If a pipe is in an area that is not exactly cold but is not heated — insulate it.

If any tap washers or cisterns are beginning to drip or run, do not wait until they've gone altogether, get them repaired now.

If you're going away during a potentially cold period, even if it's only for a night or two, leave the heating on automatic time clock so that it comes on when you're away. If you haven't got this facility, turn off all the stopcocks before you go — better still, drain down your cold water tank. This takes time but could save a lot of damage.

heating

Have your central heating, water heaters, gas fires and any

other gas appliances serviced regularly, at least once a year, preferably just after the heating season has finished

Don't rely totally on one source of heat. Keep some back-up heating just in case the main system packs up e.g. bottled gas heater, electric fire or fan heater. They can help to keep the cold at bay until you can get a repair done. But make sure the back-up appliance is safe: don't rely on an old heater that has been stuck in the loft for years.

One of the consumer advice leaflets issued by the Heating and Ventilating Contractors' Association (HVCA) is *Help yourself to a warm and trouble-free winter*.

gas

If your property is old and you're not sure how good your gas piping is, ask your gas region to check it. An old gas pipe might be susceptible to leaks.

electricity

Your electrical system should be checked to see that it is up to current standards and in a safe condition. If the wiring is old or previous owners have had various lights and sockets added to the system in a haphazard way, get a qualified electrician to check over the system and to give you a report. Then get any repairs or replacements done.

Don't overload the system by plugging too many appliances into the same socket. If you haven't got enough sockets, get some more installed.

If you use electrical appliances outside, you should have at least one residual current device to protect you from accidental electrocution when using equipment out of doors. The device can be fitted at the normal socket.

Find out where your mains electricity switch is and the fuses or miniature circuit breakers. Teach yourself how to change a fuse safely and keep a good stock of proper fuses.

roof, guttering, drains

Regularly check your roof for any slipped or missing tiles, the chimney for any loose bricks or chimney pots, a wobbly TV aerial etc. A pair of binoculars will help. If you cannot do so yourself, get a reliable person to check the roof once a year.

Get the gutters and rainwater pipes cleaned out once a year, preferably after all the leaves have fallen from the trees.

Keep all your outside drainage gullies clean; clear them out every couple of months (if you can stand it).

Do not put anything down the w.c. or sink, basins etc that might block or damage them.

general

Make sure that you have available and, most importantly, accessible in case of emergencies, the following:

○ a torch with batteries that work
○ steps or ladder to get into any loft, tank rooms etc
○ a couple of buckets and a mop or large towel in case of leaks
○ a list of contractors you can call on in an emergency.

The Royal Institution of Chartered Surveyors, jointly with BBC Television, has produced *The RICS Property Doctor Book*, diagnosing unhealthy symptoms in a house and the possible causes, and prescribing remedies. The booklet, with an insert *What will it cost?*, is available from the RICS.

calling out contractors in an emergency

An emergency means different things to different people, depending on attitude and circumstances. Generally, it's a defect that becomes suddenly apparent which requires a repair as soon as possible to minimise the risk of further damage, to make a situation safe or secure, or to cut down on extreme inconvenience. The problems increase if this occurs outside builders' and other contractors' working hours i.e.

○ between 5pm and 8am
○ saturdays and sundays
○ public holidays.

Outside normal working hours, charges increase considerably and you could be faced with a large bill for the work done.

Before you reach for the telephone to call a contractor out-of-hours, ask yourself if it is really an emergency? Try to assess the situation calmly and see if there is anything you can do to keep things tolerable until the next day or when contractors return to normal working conditions and charges.

You may be able to keep the effects within tolerable limits by turning off the mains, turning on other taps to drain the tanks, putting buckets under leaks, nailing up doors, fixing plastic over broken windows etc. Waiting a day or even a few hours could save you a lot of money.

But if the emergency is causing a lot of damage to your property — for instance, where a plumbing leak is affecting plaster ceiling and walls — your insurance company won't be impressed if you had done nothing about the problem for a day or two because you didn't want to pay emergency rates.

what to do

If you look through the Yellow Pages, you'll discover that many roofers, plumbers, glaziers etc advertise a 24-hour emergency service. Some even state that they operate 24 hours a day, 365 days a year. When you are desperate, such a service will seem very tempting but you should still take time to 'phone around if possible to try and get alternative contractors and prices.

The method of charging varies from contractor to contractor.

Many quote a cost for any part of the first hour and then a cost for any subsequent time period after that. This will usually be in addition to costs of any materials and will, of course, not include VAT.

When telephoning one of these contractors, you should ask the following questions:

○ do you have a standard call-out charge?

This will almost certainly be for the first hour of work and be higher than the charges made after the first hour.

○ is travelling time included within the call-out charge? or does the time charged begin when the operative arrives?

The 'first hour' period usually includes travelling time from the operative's home or base to your place. Depending on the distances, this could take most of your first hour.

○ will travelling costs be charged separately or are they included in the charge?

Some contractors may even make a mileage charge.

○ will VAT be additional?

○ will there be a separate charge for materials?

There almost certainly will be, the problem is how much. They would probably say it's impossible to quote over the 'phone, but if you give an accurate description of what you think has gone wrong, they may be able to give you a rough estimate.

○ when do they want to be paid?

They may want paying immediately after the work has been done or will send an invoice through later. If they do want to be paid at the time, ask whether they will take a cheque in case you do not have enough cash. Never pay in advance of the work being done.

○ will they do the job in one visit or will they have to return?

Many contractors, either through common practice or necessity, may be able to do only a certain proportion of the work at that time and may want to return the day after to complete the job. Ask them whether a separate charge will be made for this second visit and, if so, on what basis. Glaziers, for example, may just board over a broken window at night and return the next day to glaze it.

Many contractors do not quote a standard charge for the first hour or other initial time period, and say that they will have to see what the job involves. This is a common practice for roofers. In this case, find out if a call-out charge will be made if they turn up and discover that they can't do the work or you are not happy about asking them to do it.

Once they have seen the problem, they may give a firm verbal quote there and then or may say that their charges will depend on how much time they will spend doing the work. If it's the latter, ask what sort of hourly charge they will make.

If the emergency is caused by a breakdown of equipment, particularly part of the central heating system, giving accurate information improves your chances of getting a quick response to an emergency call. It may also enable the heating engineer to bring the correct spares. The HVCA suggests that before 'phoning, you should make sure that you can give the following information about your boiler:

○ make
○ model
○ heating capacity
○ information about the fault, if possible.

An HVCA service engineer can be contacted through the HVCA home heating linkline telephone number: 0345 581 158 (local charge rate).

contact lists

Not only should you try and avoid these emergencies from happening by carrying out preventive maintenance, you should also identify suitable emergency contractors now rather than waiting for an emergency to occur. Telephone a selection and ask them what are their rates, charges and conditions for emergency call-out and for normal work. One important question is how easy are they to contact outside office hours and how quickly can they respond.

Do this also with the innumerable cards pushed through the letterbox from local (and not so local) firms of 'specialist' repairers — plumbers, electricians, roofers etc plus the do-it-all chaps. Get in touch with the ones who seem most useful and check their charges and likely skills.

Make a list of the contractors you favour (and also any recommended by friends or neighbours) with their 'phone numbers and addresses and keep it next to the telephone or in some other handy place. Ring them back every few months or so to check that they are still in business, offering the same service and still charging reasonable rates.

dry rot

One of the most destructive defects that is common in older properties is dry rot. If dry rot is not spotted early, it can quickly lead to considerable deterioration and in some cases to structural collapse.

Dry rot grows on timber and feeds off the cellulose within the timber which gives the impression of sucking it dry. Although it is called dry rot, it still needs moisture to grow. In the right conditions — damp, warmth, available supply of timber — the growth gives off spores or tiny seeds by which the fungus spreads. These spores can give the surface a yellow, red or brown tinge. The spores are so small and light that they can spread for great distances on the slightest movements of air. In the worst cases, in undisturbed areas, these spores can form a thick coating over adjacent surfaces.

Another way dry rot spreads is by putting out thick vein-like strands that go in search of more wood to attack. These veins have been known to penetrate brick walls and concrete floors, and in older property can travel through the lime in the mortar.

Most dry rot attacks are usually hidden from view for most of their early period and only become apparent when the wood it is feeding off visibly deteriorates. Wood that has been affected by dry rot usually shrinks and splits, both along and across the 'grain' so that the wood splits into what looks like cubes; the wood becomes lighter in weight and loses its resinous smell. Its appearance is very similar to charred wood but without the black colouring.

Dry rot usually begins in concealed places where it is damp, warm and unventilated. One of the most common locations especially in older properties, is the skirting board to the ground floor. Here, the dry rot will usually gain a hold from the back of the skirting before any characteristic cracking shows on the room side. The surface of the wood, especially if it's painted will become warped, wavy, or irregular.

Another sign is the distinctive dry rot smell. It smells very musty, like old damp books in the cellar. Many surveyors can recognise an attack when they walk into the affected room just by breathing the air.

keeping your property in good order

In respect of dry rot, the main enemy is dampness. So you should

○ keep all gutters, rainwater pipes, drain pipes, hot and cold water pipes in good condition; repair any leak as soon as possible, don't leave it — dry rot can start very quickly
○ repair any loose or missing slates on the roof, and valley gutters and flashing around base of chimneys
○ make sure that there is enough fresh air ventilation beneath ground floors, in basements and roof spaces; this will help to prevent the build-up of damp conditions.

regular inspection

Rot will start where timber is in contact with or in close proximity to damp materials. At six-monthly intervals, you should inspect any areas of your house where these features might coincide. Typical locations would be

○ cellar or basement especially where floor joists or staircases are next to brick walls
○ the skirting boards at the junction of the ground floor and wall
○ any wood panelling on ground floor or basement walls
○ roof timbers where they are built into or onto brick walls
○ timber window frames and sills.

Look out for visual signs (in its first phase, dry rot often produces large expanses of a fluffy cottonwool-like growth) and sniff around for the musty smell. Press the end of a small screwdriver or knife against the timber with firm pressure (don't stab at it). If it sinks into the timber quite easily to a depth of, say, $\frac{1}{2}$ an inch, you've got problems.

If you suspect that there is dry rot, call in a timber treatment firm to carry out a survey of the affected area and to produce a report recommending the necessary remedial measures.

timber treatment

In many older properties, the structural timbers in the roof and floors may have been affected by either dry or wet rot or by woodworm. There are many different types of each, some worse than others; unless remedial treatment is carried out, further deterioration will occur and, in the most dramatic cases, lead to structural collapse.

With dry rot, because it has the ability to spread far and wide, all the affected timber has to be cut out and replaced and the adjacent construction treated or sprayed with special chemicals. Where an attack is next to a wall, plaster may have to be removed so that brickwork can be treated because the strands of the dry rot can penetrate very deep.

Although woodworm is not usually as damaging as dry rot, unless the affected timber and surrounding area is treated with special chemicals, the woodworm will spread.

When looking for an expert to come to inspect and advise on any apparently infected timber on your property, ask the British Wood Preserving Association for a list of their members in your area. The BWPA is the trade association for companies specialising in remedial timber treatment and repair. It has a detailed code of practice that its members must follow. Or you can contact direct one of the nationally-known firms who advertise widely and/or have regional offices throughout the country.

A surveyor who has the letters CTIS after his name has the additional qualification of the certificate for timber infestation surveyors, awarded by The Institute of Wood Science. The syllabus for the qualifying examination covers building construction, structure of woods, survey techniques, report writing, entomology and mycology (life cycles of specified fungi), timber preservation, and legal responsibilities.

inspection

Prior to a quotation, a timber treatment company will want to carry out a full inspection or survey of your property to determine the extent and type of work required.

The inspection will not normally exceed the 'instructions' given by you. This means that the surveyor or inspector will look only at the areas that you specifically request. So, before you ask a company to carry out a survey, you must consider the extent of the work you require. For instance, if you have an outbreak of dry rot in your rear kitchen, consider asking them to look not only at that problem but at your home as a whole. If you own an older property, it is more likely to have rot and/or woodworm problems. So, ask the surveyor to report on the whole house not just a specific area.

To ensure that the quotation is accurate, the survey should be quite extensive. The surveyor should want to crawl beneath your floorboards, climb into your roof space and poke into the most inaccessible areas of your home. The surveyor should come supplied with sufficient equipment for the survey, including portable ladder, tools for lifting floorboards, torch, overalls etc; you must ensure that you provide as much access as possible. This may have to include lifting fitted carpets, moving furniture etc especially where ground level timber floors meet the walls.

Be wary of the surveyor who doesn't seem too keen to get his head beneath the floorboards. A quote based on a superficial inspection may lead to extra work once the job begins if all the defects were not discovered in the first place.

Dampness plays an important part: the surveyor should identify the sources of this dampness and suggest work that will be needed to cure it. Having this work carried out will probably be a condition of any guarantee for the timber treatment.

the report
Following the survey, you should receive a full report outlining the condition of the property at the time of inspection, the remedial works required and a quote for the work. This report should include

○ the name of the inspecting company and the date of the inspection
○ written confirmation of your instructions to them
○ adequate information so that rooms of different areas of the property can be identified. (Ideally, sketch plans or other drawings should be included so that the area affected and the extent of the treatment needed is very clear.)
○ a clear indication of what areas are going to be treated, the cleaning and application methods and the type of preservative to be used.

The report should have a clear statement about who is responsible for any preparatory works. Many timber specialists operate as sub-contractors and expect you to get other builders to hack off any plaster, replace any structural timbers. If it affects kitchen and/or bathroom areas, it could involve taking off and refixing bath, sink, cupboards etc. Other firms may offer this service themselves.

The report should include warnings about your responsibility to prevent damage to your fixtures and fittings. For instance, you will need to move all your floor coverings and furniture out and, in some cases, will have to wait a few days before you can move them back in. If several areas of your house are affected, this could present you with furniture storage problems.

The actual quote should clearly relate to the work outlined in the body of the report. It may include a guarantee for a set number of years in case of recurrence of the insect or fungal attack in the areas treated.

One point to watch is the making good or repair work that may be associated with the work. If a timber treatment firm offers to replace floor joists, boards, skirtings and do the replastering, ask them to clarify who will be doing it — their own operatives or some local sub-contractor? If you are organising this aspect of the work with a builder, take the usual precautions to ensure that both parts of the work are well co-ordinated.

preparations

The chemicals used for timber treatment are potentially dangerous pesticides. All the products used must have been cleared as 'safe for use' under the government's pesticides safety precautions scheme. Ask the contractor for evidence of this.

Because of the potential dangers, certain preparations will have to be carried out:

○ removal of all floor coverings, furniture, soft furnishings etc; in loft spaces, water tanks must be protected with plastic sheeting, all thermal insulation either removed or rolled up and protected with plastic sheeting

○ electrical circuits in the treatment area should be isolated and protected to stop the treatment fluid from entering them; if you still have rubber sheathed electrical wiring, this could be badly affected by the treatment and so should be well protected — or replaced

○ before any treatment is started, warning notices should be posted stating that chemical treatments are being applied; smoking should be banned and no naked lights allowed. This includes the pilot light on any gas central heating or water heater or cooker

○ anyone who isn't involved in the application of the treatment should be kept away from the area being treated; this may involve moving everyone out of the house for a few days.

One major contractor recommends the following precautions:

"FOR A PERIOD OF NOT LESS THAN 48 HOURS
○ ensure that all rooms in which work has been carried out are thoroughly and continuously ventilated
○ avoid the use of such rooms for sleeping, especially for young children, elderly people or any person susceptible to respiratory problems
○ do not return fish, caged birds and other pets to treated rooms
○ do not expose unwrapped foodstuffs in treated rooms
○ avoid skin contact with treated surfaces.

FOR A PERIOD OF NOT LESS THAN 14 DAYS
○ leave open the hatch or doors to treated roof voids, lofts, cellars and other treated spaces to provide ventilation
○ make sure that smoking is not permitted in treated areas, nor other naked flames such as blowlamps etc. Make sure that anyone entering the treated area is aware of this
○ make sure that the warning notices are displayed in the treated areas for a period of 14 days."

damp proofing

Damp proof course installation and timber treatment are very common repairs in older properties. They are generally carried out by specialist firms and many firms will deal with both problems.

The ground outside most buildings in this country is almost always damp. Because the walls of houses are generally drier than the ground they are built on, the dampness is 'sucked' up into the wall like water into a sponge.

To prevent this dampness from entering the dwelling, a damp proof course is installed within the thickness of the wall. In the past, this consisted of two rows of dense waterproof bricks or a thinner layer of roofing slates within a mortar course. Over time, these damp proof courses break down and allow dampness to pass into the dwelling affecting the plaster and decorations and creating unhealthy living conditions.

chemical damp proof course (dpc)

One of the most common methods of solving this problem is by installing a new chemical damp proof course. This involves injecting chemicals into the wall. When the chemical dries, this prevents further dampness rising and so the wall slowly dries out. The chemical is injected through a number of holes drilled at regular intervals into the walls from the inside or sometimes from the outside, or with thicker walls, from both sides.

The rising dampness brings with it other chemicals or 'salts' from the ground. These are deposited within the brickwork and plaster as the rising dampness dries out within the room. These salts are 'hygroscopic' which means that they attract moisture from the air and cause the brickwork or plaster around them to become damp. So, even if the injection of chemical has stopped the rising dampness, because these hygroscopic salts have been left within the wall, dampness could reappear whenever the moisture level of the room rises to a sufficiently high level.

It is therefore common practice to hack off the plaster that has been affected and replaster with a new plaster that has an additive that prevents these salts from entering the new plaster. Walls are usually replastered to a height of one metre from the floor.

the specialist firms

There is a great deal of variation between companies offering this service. If you invite several different ones to quote for work on your house, you may find that each one recommends something different.

Most of the contractors who specialise in this area of work have properly trained their operatives and built up a certain level of expertise. But this is not always the case: the equipment for this work can be hired quite easily and a general builder may offer this service. To be sure of a basic standard of work, the contractor should be a member of the British Chemical Dampcourse Association, the trade association, which has a code of practice that all its members must abide by.

the quotation and the work

You should ask two or three companies to quote. You won't have the technical knowledge to define the extent of the work yourself. The companies will send their 'surveyor' around who will prepare a report on the property identifying those areas that, in his opinion, require treatment.

Quotations or estimates can be expected to be free of charge, but 'free surveys' do not necessarily give sufficient time for complete analysis of the problems. A full comprehensive report and dampness analysis programme can be obtained (for a charge) from a qualified certificated remedial dampcoursing surveyor (CRDS) who has passed a national examination organised by the British Chemical Dampcourse Association.

Most chemical damp proof course firms also carry out remedial timber treatment work as well. Their reports, unless you specifically request them not to do so, will almost certainly make comment on the condition of the existing timbers.

The way the firms operate may differ. Some may consider

themselves as 'sub-contractors' and so require a general builder to be around to provide them with all the 'attendance' they
require. This could include

○ taking off and refixing skirtings, hacking off plaster and
  carting away debris etc.
○ if the work affects kitchen or bathrooms, the builder will
  need to take out bath, basins, pipework, WC, for access for
  injection and replastering, and replace them all when the
  work has been finished
○ any electrical wiring will have to be moved temporarily.

Other damp proofing firms will carry out this 'attendance'
work themselves and include it in their quote, so make sure
that you know what work the contractor is including.

Although many of the firms carry out the work using their
own employees, many others use sub-contractors. They might
do the injection themselves but get another contractor in to do
the plastering. Although this is not necessarily a bad thing,
you need to know that there is good control and communication between the two.

If you are having other work carried out at the same time, the
specialist firm or the general builder may suggest that the
general builder should carry out the replastering in accordance
with the specification supplied by the specialist. You should
think very carefully before agreeing to this because the specialist will not guarantee the treatment unless the plastering is
done exactly in accordance with the original requirements.

the guarantee
Most dpc firms give a guarantee with their work, usually for 20
or 30 years. This may seem very generous and reassuring but
the guarantee is not all that comprehensive.

The guarantee will cover only the areas that have been
treated by the contractor. So, if rising damp occurs in an area

not injected, it will not be covered by any guarantee even if the firm's surveyor said that that area didn't need a dpc in the first place.

Most guarantees will state that the property should be kept in good order and well maintained especially the guttering, window and door sills, and other parts where defects could cause dampness in the walls. If you call back a dpc firm on the guarantee because you notice dampness after a few years and you've got a leaking gutter or cracked rainwater pipe in the vicinity, the firm will probably blame that defect for causing the dampness. (Penetrating dampness can gravitate in masonry and accumulate dampness above an efficient dampcourse, giving an impression of rising damp or dpc failure.)

If the replastering has been carried out by another builder and dampness is in evidence, the damp proofing firm will probably take a sample of the plaster away for accurate analysis. If it's not an exact match to the plaster type that they orginally recommended, they may deny liability and blame whoever replastered the walls.

Even if the original contractor admits that the damp proof course has failed, the guarantee is usually limited to the cost of the original treatment. In other works, they will offer to re-inject the affected wall but give nothing towards the redecorations and the disturbance.

The firm may charge an inspection fee to come and look at the alleged problem. If the dpc proves to be at fault, this is returned but if they consider that they are not responsible, then they'll hold on to it. The fee is usually around £20 to £30 (for this, you should expect a fully comprehensive analysis and report).

insurance for guarantees

The Guarantee Protection Trust, an independent organisation, an offspring of the BCDA and the BWPA, offers an insurance scheme specifically designed for their timber treatment and dampcourse guarantees.

If a contractor has gone bankrupt or ceased to trade for some other reason or cannot meet a claim under the original guarantee, the GPT will stand in the place of the contractor and honour the guarantee. The scheme is confined to members of the BCDA and BWPA. Only firms which are members of both associations can use the guarantee protection scheme for both kinds of work: timber treatment and chemical damp proof course.

You, the customer, have to pay a £10 fee for guarantee protection for either timber treatment or chemical damp proof course (i.e. £20 for both) for contracts up to £10,000 before VAT.

Membership of trade organisations

If a firm claims to be a member of a particular trade organisation, you can check whether this is really so by getting in touch with the association's head office. Addresses of some that are relevant to building work are given on pages 211 to 216.

A trade association offers many advantages to its members; that is the prime objective of most associations. Benefits for the ordinary householder/customer will vary, depending on the association and the member firm.

Whether it's worth employing a builder or specialist contractor because he belongs to that industry's trade association will depend on the circumstances. Bear in mind that trade associations exist to promote the interests of their own members. Over the last few years, many associations have realised that unreputable trading within their industry is a serious threat to their members' interests, and they have formulated customer protection practices. A number of these are useful in that they do offer some measure of protection to the ordinary customer.

If things are beginning to go off the rails with the firm you are employing, the trade association's intervention might just be sufficient to prevent a disaster. Where a dispute or problem is more serious, however, their disputes procedure may not cope.

organisations for specific trades

Of the many trades within the building/construction industry, some provide essential services, others are important for improving and maintaining property to an acceptable standard, others fulfil a more cosmetic function. Whichever you are drawing on, you want to be able to rely on a high standard of competence, integrity and efficiency. There are few objective criteria to help, but membership of some trade organisation should provide an element of reassurance.

Here is some information about some of the trade bodies that you may like to refer to for the work you are having done.

electrical work

The overriding issue with any electrical work is to ensure safety, for installers and users alike. It is not just vested interest that prompts electrical contractors to urge the uninitiated not to meddle with electrical installations and fittings. Unless you are 100 per cent certain of what you are doing, there can be dire consequences for you, your partner, children, visitors and subsequent occupiers.

For electrical work on your house, there are two regulatory bodies which set standards for their members.

The **National Inspection Council for Electrical Installation Contracting** (NICEIC) is an independent consumer safety body whose concern is the protection of users of electrical installations. The NICEIC has established a Roll of Approved Electrical Contractors (there are now over 11,000 of them) whose work conforms to the IEE (Institution of Electrical Engineers) Wiring Regulations and related BSI codes of practice. An electrical contractor is only allowed on the NICEIC Roll if he uses materials of good quality, is totally proficient in electrical installation work, is adequately supervised or supervises others to a high degree. And he must maintain such standards to remain on the Roll. Approved contractors are inspected on a regular basis by the NICEIC to ensure that they are maintaining the required standards of workmanship and safety.

Each approved contractor must issue an NICEIC completion certificate for every job he carries out, confirming that the work has been done in compliance with the required regulations. You should make sure that you get this certificate from the contractor before agreeing that the electrical work has been properly finished.

The NICEIC will investigate complaints about the safety or workmanship of electrical installation carried out by one of its approved contractors, and in some circumstances, guarantees to appoint another approved contractor to finish the work or correct the faults.

The trade association for the electrical contracting industry is the **Electrical Contractors' Association**. Companies which are members will have satisfied the association of their technical competence and commercial integrity. Employees of member firms must have been fully trained and be fully qualified. A register of members is issued annually by the ECA.

The association offers customers of members certain safeguards and guarantees which cover members' work and contracts. If a complaint of poor or unfinished work is held to be justified, the work will be put right at once, at no cost to the customer. There is a contract completion guarantee whereby if a member fails to complete a contract, the job will be completed by another contractor at the original contract price.

The ECA offers to give advice and help on design and layout of wiring and fittings, but does not enter into any dispute between contractor and customer on prices; it strongly recommends customers to obtain estimates of cost of work whenever possible.

The **Electrical Contractors' Association of Scotland** has a code of good practice for electrical installations, drawn up with the stated aim of ensuring the best possible relationship between a firm and its customers. There is also a set of 'fair and reasonable' conditions intended to provide the best possible service at realistic and reasonable cost. This standard set of conditions is available to all members of the association but can be modified, and there is no obligation to use them. The code and conditions apply to electrical contracting work undertaken by member firms directly for customers that is not regulated by other building contracts or sub-contracts.

A procedure is laid down for customer complaints that cannot be resolved between the two parties. For the ECA of S to assist, the complaint must be made in writing to the association within 12 months of the work being carried out.

On small jobs where the payment was to be made after the work was completed but the contractor goes into liquidation during the course of the job, the ECA of S's code recognises that the customer's problem is not so much financial as one of inconvenience. The association undertakes to get another member firm to complete the work as quickly as possible, with the minimum disruption, at a price as close as possible to the original price.

plumbing

Unlike many other countries, there is no statutory control in the UK over the use of the title 'plumber' or 'plumbing contractor' so anyone can set up as a plumber without proof of competence or qualification. If you come upon a plumber who is not a member of any trade or professional body, ask whether he has any training qualifications, such as a City & Guilds certificate.

The **Institute of Plumbing** is a professional association registered as a charity, not an employers' trade association. It maintains a register of plumbers (currently, about 12,000 are registered) which is monitored under the British Standards Institution's PRIMA (Public Register Inspection Maintenance Assessment) scheme. Registration with the Institute of Plumbing is voluntary and is intended "to enable the public to distinguish plumbers who have given evidence of their competency and who undertake to act responsibly . . . and to raise the efficiency and status of plumbers."

Registered plumbers who are self-employed or in business may be listed in the *Business Directory of Registered Plumbers*, published annually by the Institute, and available at citizens advice bureaux, major public libraries and other relevant information points. Currently, some 5000 are listed in the Directory.

Each registered plumber should display a certificate of registration and carry an annually renewable pocket card as proof of registration.

The Institute will investigate complaints against any registered plumber where there is evidence to suggest that he may have contravened his undertaking to act competently and responsibly but will not intervene in a contractual dispute such as the price charged for plumbing work. The ultimate sanction is removal from the register for serious cases, although this does not prevent those so removed from continuing to call themselves 'plumber'.

The plumber's role nowadays spans that of other specialist services, mainly in the heating sphere, and there are composite bodies — for example, the **National Association of Plumbing, Heating and Mechanical Services Contractors** and the **Scottish and Northern Ireland Plumbing Employers' Federation.** Members are vetted for competence in installation work and sound business before being accepted on the register.

The associations have a code of fair trading, approved by the Office of Fair Trading, to which all members have to conform. This code is intended for jobbing and small estimate work including central heating, that is not carried out under the standard conditions of contract in the construction industry. The code includes a standard set of 'fair and reasonable conditions between firms and customers', but a contractor is at liberty to disregard or to modify these standard conditions to match any particular circumstances.

The code also lays down principles for dealing with customer complaints. The association sees failure of communications and lack of understanding of the other's position as being a cause for complaints arising. The code recommends that the contractor should try to keep the customer informed on all 'salient' matters and that complaints should be sympathetically listened to and a courteous explanation given. The association is prepared to assist in resolving complaints by bringing the firm and the customer together in the first instance. The association states that it cannot advise customers about the amounts charged by firms or the time taken to do the work. The most that they will do is to say whether or not the account seems reasonable — but they admit that they might have difficulty doing even this.

roofing

The **National Federation of Roofing Contractors** is the trade organisation for firms primarily involved with roofing operations including slating and tiling, flat roofing and mastic asphalting (through the autonomous Mastic Asphalt Council and Employers Federation). Contractors have to satisfy the Federation's standards before they are allowed to join. These include a responsible trading record for a minimum of two or three years; inspection of work in progress and work recently completed; inspection of premises and stock yard.

The Federation claims that employing a NFRC member will bring the following advantages: free inspection by an experienced roofing surveyor; free written estimate in accordance with the Federation's guidelines so that the customer can clearly see the work to be undertaken and the conditions of the contract; first class materials complying with British Standards, where appropriate; workmanship in accordance with BSI codes of practice.

The National Federation of Roofing Contractors and the Mastic Asphalt Council have an insurance-backed guarantee scheme to give cover for 10 years so that if the original contractor has ceased trading within that period and a defect or failure in the roofing occurs, remedial work will be carried out under the guarantee. For domestic roofing, the customer (you) has to pay a premium of £9 for this defective workmanship solvency guarantee insurance (for the Mastic Asphalt Council guarantee, the fee is 1.5% of the contract price). You have to specify at the outset that you want this insurance and you can only have the protection if the firm of contractors you are using partakes in the guarantee insurance scheme for all its work — it is not available for one-off occasional jobs.

central heating

When you have decided to put in central heating for the first time or to change your existing system, you will need to get advice from a heating engineer and/or plumber (and perhaps also an electrician). Competent plumbing firms undertake central heating installation and some central heating firms offer plumbing services.

Employing a competent heating engineer is particularly important if you are considering putting in one of the pressurised (unvented) domestic hot water systems which are potentially dangerous in hands of amateurs and cowboys.

There are British Standards covering domestic central heating (for example, BS 5449 part 1) and the British Board of Agrément has certification for unvented hot water storage systems and an approval system for installers of the systems.

The established organisations covering heating work are the Heating and Ventilating Contractors' Association, the National Association of Plumbing, Heating and Mechanical Services Contractors. The Scottish and Northern Ireland Plumbing Employers' Federation, The Institute of Plumbing.

Member firms of the **Heating and Ventilating Contractors' Association** must not be tied exclusively to any one type of heating system and must agree to offer the HVCA "double" guarantee on new domestic central heating installations. This guarantees for one year that the central heating will perform in accordance with the specification; it also covers safety, quality of design, quality of workmanship and quality of materials.

There is a complaints procedure via HVCA if a dispute cannot be resolved between a contractor and a customer. If the contractor ultimately fails to rectify a fault notified during the guarantee period, the HVCA will commission another member firm to undertake the necessary completion or alteration (at no cost to the householder).

The HVCA lays down a code of practice for its members, applying to all forms of work not covered by the double guarantee. This normally means repair, service and maintenance of an existing system or equipment. The code covers related activities such as electrical, gas and water connections which form an integral part of the main central heating work. The code encourages good communication with the customer and gives guidance on such matters as standards of workmanship and materials, costs, payment terms, settlement of disputes. A copy should be provided by an HVCA member with all quotations to customers.

The HVCA also offers an extended warranty scheme, providing insurance for 3 years or 5 years (including the one-year guarantee period), on payment of a single premium. An application form is available from HVCA members.

Explanatory leaflets issued by the HVCA include *How do we do it for the price?*, *What you should look for in a central heating quotation*, *Your guide to central heating with a double guarantee*.

insulation

Specific areas of insulation (lofts, walls, draughts) are covered by separate trade associations, four of them based at the same address and under the same directorship.

The **National Association of Loft Insulation Contractors** is the association for firms dealing primarily with loft insulation. Member firms have to abide by a code of professional practice including a warranty that the member will investigate any complaint made by a customer and make good any defects arising solely from faulty materials or workmanship, provided that the firm is notified in writing within six months of the completion date. In the event of a dispute, there is an arbitration scheme with the association's committee acting as arbitrator.

Adding cladding to a building in order to insulate and renovate the external walls is a fairly new industry, involving specialist designers and contractors. The **External Wall Insulation Association** has been established by designers of wall insulation systems in order to set and maintain uniform standards for the materials and methods used. The aims of the EWIA include "to establish good technical, ethical and legal standards for the industry . . . and to give impartial advice". So, you should be given accurate information and objective advice. The code of professional practice encourages members to give preference to companies and designers who are also members of the EWIA. A technical standard, to which member firms must adhere, has been produced by the industry in the form of a detailed specification, covering system certification, testing procedures, component parts and performance criteria.

If your house was built since the 1930s, it will probably have a cavity wall. If you are having heating/insulation problems, you may be advised that cavity wall insulation is required. The British Board of Agrément certification procedure covers cavity wall insulation materials and installers.

Firms carrying out cavity insulation work using the three commonly used materials/processes of foam, bead and mineral wool, may belong to the **National Cavity Insulation Association**, which can provide information on product types and processes. If you have been contacted direct by a contractor offering cavity wall insulation or you have got in touch with a firm by responding to an advertisement, you should check whether the firm is a recognised contractor and a member of the NCIA. The NCIA has a code of professional practice for its members to comply with. For instance, a member firm "is obliged to maintain as a minimum the technical standards

legally required for product and workmanship, and to uphold
the laws and statutory regulations governing cavity wall insulation in the UK" and to use 'all reasonable care' to avoid
intentionally imparting false or misleading information to any
customer. A member firm must initially do a proper survey of
a building to check whether it is suitable for cavity wall
insulation (and tell you if it is not) and not give a firm price or
quotation before doing a quantity survey of the property.

In addition, the NCIA offers a customer protection plan. This
includes provision for the association — at its discretion — to
attempt to mediate in the event of an unresolved dispute
between a member firm and a customer. If a member goes into
liquidation and a problem arises attributable to the ex-
member's workmanship, the NCIA may make an ex-gratia
payment out of its contingency fund or may finance remedial
work, provided the defect or failure is established as being due
to faulty cavity wall insulation. You have to pay a fee (set by the
NCIA) towards a surveyor's fee for inspecting and reporting on
your property; this is refunded if the problem does prove to be
attributable to the cavity wall insulation.

The **Cavity Foam Bureau** is the specialist association for the
cavity foam insulation industry. The Bureau operates under
the requirements of the British Standards Institution for
injected cavity wall insulation systems. Members of the CFB are
all registered with the BSI; raw materials suppliers can only
supply contractors approved by and registered with the BSI.

The Cavity Foam Bureau offers technical advice on cavity
foam insulation and will investigate a complaint against a
member and mediate should a dispute remain unresolved. It
operates a domestic defective workmanship solvency guarantee insurance similar to that available through members of the
National Federation of Roofing Contractors. The contractor
can only allow you to take advantage of this guarantee insur-

ance if he has undertaken to offer it for all his work. If so, you may get the cost (£9) presented to you as a separate item on the bill or it may be included in the overall price as part of his 'overheads'.

There is also an association for firms who do draught proofing or weather stripping: the **Draught Proofing Advisory Association**. The association's code of professional practice contains the usual clauses, with provision for investigating complaints by a member of the public against any member firm, taking 'necessary action' to rectify the situation, with the ultimate arbiter a member of the association's council. And the onus of proof is very much on the customer.

The Energy Efficiency Office of the Department of Energy produces a number of leaflets in a Monergy Fact File series, giving advice and information on insulation and draught-proofing, heating systems and controls, double glazing (available free from Blackhorse Road, London SE99 6TT).

glazing

One of the most sophisticated and established home-selling industries is the double glazing or replacement window firm. The Office of Fair Trading has been closely concerned with this industry and has published a leaflet *Double glazing*, to counteract and help avoid problems. It states that "Reputable firms, — who carry out the greater part of this work — are concerned that for some people, double glazing is associated with a long list of ills. The main problems have been high pressure salesmanship, delays in installation, unexpected price increases, poor workmanship and lost deposits."

The **Glass and Glazing Federation** is the main trade association for double glazing companies. (Any salesperson from a firm which is a member of the GGF should carry a plastic identity card as proof that the firm is a member.) The GGF has drawn up a code of ethical practice, in consultation with the Office of Fair Trading, to which all its members must adhere. This covers all aspects of trading with consumers, from advertising and selling, installation and quality standards, to after-sales service and complaints handling. The industry has developed its own contract terms or terms of estimate, which are now fairly consistent among member firms of the GGF and which include a number of clauses resulting from discussions with the OFT.

It is normal practice with double glazing contractors to ask for a deposit of between about 10% and 25% of the contract price. The GGF runs a deposit indemnity fund so that you shouldn't lose your deposit even if the firm you are dealing with goes out of business. If a GGF member is unable to do the work and has taken a deposit, the GGF will arrange for another member firm to do the work at a 'fair market rate' (which could be higher than the original quotation) less the deposit you originally paid. The limit on the deposit covered is 25% of the contract price where new windows are being fitted.

Where a dispute between a GGF member and the customer cannot be resolved, the GGF has drawn up a simplified arbitration scheme with the Chartered Institute of Arbitrators, based on written submissions (no personal hearing), undertaking to achieve a decision within three months of the original referral. There is a registration fee (of £20 to £30) payable by the customer.

One of the features of the glazing industry is that a builder is not required for a large part of the work — and some may not be sufficiently trained nor up to date with materials, techniques and processes to carry out specialist glazing work. Your contract will be direct with the glazing firm, with membership of the Glass and Glazing Federation as the criterion for quality and satisfaction.

epilogue

Despite the difficulties this book warns about, there are satisfied customers whose success stories testify that they have had the good fortune and/or sufficient knowledge to choose one of the best of builders and more sympathetic of professionals to accomplish the work they wanted done in the way they wanted.

One way to safeguard the outcome of your scheme is to use someone — professional or builder, electrician or plumber or glazier — who has qualified for membership of a reputable trade or professional organisation, so that he or she is in some way answerable to colleagues and/or peers as well as to you for any lapses.

The following are the addresses of organisations mentioned in this book, with a few others likely to be relevant for work you may be embarking on.

addresses

Association of Consultant Architects
7 Park Street, Bristol BS1 5NF ☎ 0272 293379

Barnsley Consumer and Environmental Services
Regent House, Regent Street, Barnsley S70 2TG
☎ 0226 733232

BEC Building Trust
18 Mansfield Street, London W1M 9FG ☎ 01-580 6306

Birmingham Environmental Services Department
4th floor, 120 Edmund Street, Birmingham B3 2EZ
☎ 021-235 2330

British Board of Agrément
PO Box 195, Bucknalls Lane, Garston, Watford,
Herts WD2 7NG ☎ 0923 670844

British Chemical Dampcourse Association
16a Whitchurch Road, Pangbourne, Berks RG8 7BP
☎ 07357 3799

British Institute of Architectural Technicians
397 City Road, London EC1V 1NE ☎ 01-278 2206

British Standards Institution
2 Park Street, London W1A 2BS ☎ 01-629 9000

British Wood Preserving Association
6 The Office Village, 4 Romford Road, London E15 4EA
☎ 01-519 2588

Building Centres
26 Store Street, London WC1E 7BT ☎ 01-637 1022
35 King Street, Bristol BS1 4DZ ☎ 0272 260264
113–115 Portland Street, Manchester M1 6FB ☎ 061 236 9802
131 West Nile Street, Glasgow G1 2RX ☎ 041 333 9701

Building Employers Confederation
82 New Cavendish Street, London W1M 8AD ☎ 01-580 5588

Building Research Establishment
Bucknalls Lane, Garston, Watford, Herts, WD2 7JR
☎ 0923 894040

Cavity Foam Bureau
PO Box 79, Oldbury, Warley, West Midlands B69 4PW
☎ 021-544 4949

Chartered Institute of Arbitrators
International Arbitration Centre, 75 Cannon Street,
London EC4N 5BH ☎ 01-236 8761

Chartered Institute of Building
  Englemere, Kings Ride, Ascot, Berks SL5 8BJ ☎ 0990 23355

Draught Proofing Advisory Association Ltd
  PO Box 12, Haslemere, Surrey GU27 3AN ☎ 0428 54011

Electrical Contractors' Association
  ESCA House, 34 Palace Court, London W2 4HY ☎ 01-229 1266

Electrical Contractors' Association of Scotland
  23 Heriot Row, Edinburgh EH3 6EW ☎ 031-225 7221

External Wall Insulation Association
  PO Box 12, Haslemere, Surrey GU27 3AN ☎ 0428 54011

Faculty of Architects and Surveyors
  15 St Mary Street, Chippenham, Wilts SN15 3JN ☎ 0249 655398

Federation of Master Builders
  Gordon Fisher House, 33 John Street, London WC1N 2BB
  ☎ 01-242 7583

Glass and Glazing Federation
  44–48 Borough High Street, London SE1 1XB ☎ 01-403 7177

Guarantee Protection Trust
  PO Box 77, 27 London Road, High Wycombe,
  Bucks HP11 1BW ☎ 0494 447049

Guild of Master Craftsmen
  166 High Street, Lewes, East Sussex BN7 1XU ☎ 0273 478449

Guild of Surveyors
  161 Queens Road, Oldham, Lancs OL8 2BA ☎ 061-627 2389

Heating and Ventilating Contractors' Association
  ESCA House, 34 Palace Court, London W2 4JG ☎ 01-229 2488
  23 Heriot Row, Edinburgh EH3 6EW ☎ 031-225 8212

Incorporated Association of Architects and Surveyors
Jubilee House, Billing Brook Road, Weston Favell,
Northampton NN3 4NW ☎ 0604 404121

Incorporated Society of Valuers and Auctioneers
3 Cadogan Gate, London SW1X 0AS ☎ 01-235 2282

Institute of Building Control
21 High Street, Ewell, Epsom, Surrey KT17 1SB ☎ 01-393 6860

Institute of Plumbing
64 Station Lane, Hornchurch, Essex RM12 6NB ☎ 04024 72791

Institute of Wood Science
Stocking Lane, Hughenden Valley, High Wycombe,
Bucks HP14 4NU ☎ 0240 245374

Institution of Electrical Engineers
Savoy Place, London WC2R 0BL ☎ 01-240 1871

Institution of Structural Engineers
11 Upper Belgrave Street, London SW1X 8BH ☎ 01-235 4535

Kitchen Specialists Association
8 St Bernard's Crescent, Edinburgh EH4 1NP ☎ 031-332 8884

Mastic Asphalt Council and Employers Federation
24 Weymouth Street, London W1N 3FA ☎ 01-436 0102

National Association of Loft Insulation Contractors
PO Box 12, Haslemere, Surrey GU27 3AN ☎ 0428 54011

National Association of Plumbing, Heating and Mechanical
Services Contractors
6 Gate Street, London WC2A 3HX ☎ 01-405 2678

National Cavity Insulation Association
PO Box 12, Haslemere, Surrey GU27 3AN ☎ 0428 54011

National Federation of Roofing Contractors
24 Weymouth Street, London W1N 3FA ☎ 01-436 0387

National Home Improvement Council
26 Store Street, London WC1E 7BT ☎ 01-636 2562

National Inspection Council for Electrical
Installation Contracting
Vintage House, 36–37 Albert Embankment, London SE1 7UJ
☎ 01-582 7746

Office of Fair Trading
Chancery House, Chancery Lane, London WC2A 1SP
☎ 01-242 2858

Royal Incorporation of Architects in Scotland
15 Rutland Square, Edinburgh EH1 2BE ☎ 031-229 7205

Royal Institute of British Architects
66 Portland Place, London W1N 4AD ☎ 01-580 5533

Royal Institution of Chartered Surveyors
12 Great George Street, London SW1P 3AD ☎ 01-222 7000
9 Manor Place, Edinburgh EH3 7DN ☎ 031-225 7078

Royal Society of Ulster Architects
2 Mount Charles, Belfast BT7 1NZ ☎ 0232 323760

Royal Town Planning Institute
26 Portland Place, London W1N 4BE ☎ 01-636 9107
15 Rutland Square, Edinburgh EH1 2BE ☎ 031-337 3423

Scottish Building Employers Federation
13 Woodside Crescent, Glasgow G3 7UP ☎ 041-332 7144

Scottish and Northern Ireland Plumbing
Employers' Federation
2 Walker Street, Edinburgh EH3 7LB ☎ 031-225 2255

Society of Architects in Wales
75a Llandennis Road, Rhydypennau, Cardiff CF2 6EE
☎ 0222 762215

Society for the Protection of Ancient Buildings
37 Spital Square, London E1 6DY ☎ 01-377 1644

Society of Surveying Technicians
Drayton House, 30 Gordon Street, London WC1H OBH
☎ 01-388 8008

Women and Manual Trades
52-54 Featherstone Street, London EC1Y 8RT ☎ 01-251 9192

Index